Getting Skills Right: Good Practice in Adapting to Changing Skill Needs

A PERSPECTIVE ON FRANCE, ITALY, SPAIN, SOUTH AFRICA AND THE UNITED KINGDOM

OECD

BETTER POLICIES FOR BETTER LIVES

This work is published under the responsibility of the Secretary-General of the OECD. The opinions expressed and arguments employed herein do not necessarily reflect the official views of OECD member countries.

This document and any map included herein are without prejudice to the status of or sovereignty over any territory, to the delimitation of international frontiers and boundaries and to the name of any territory, city or area.

Please cite this publication as:
OECD (2017), *Getting Skills Right: Good Practice in Adapting to Changing Skill Needs: A Perspective on France, Italy, Spain, South Africa and the United Kingdom*, OECD Publishing, Paris.
http://dx.doi.org/10.1787/9789264277892-en

ISBN 978-92-64-27788-5 (print)
ISBN 978-92-64-27789-2 (PDF)

Series: Getting Skills Right
ISSN 2520-6117 (print)
ISSN 2520-6125 (online)

The statistical data for Israel are supplied by and under the responsibility of the relevant Israeli authorities. The use of such data by the OECD is without prejudice to the status of the Golan Heights, East Jerusalem and Israeli settlements in the West Bank under the terms of international law.

Photo credits: Cover © Cell phone: ©Creative Commons/Alfredo Hernandez, clock: ©Creative Commons/Hakan

Corrigenda to OECD publications may be found on line at: *www.oecd.org/about/publishing/corrigenda.htm*.

Foreword

Across countries, tackling skill mismatch and skill shortages is a major challenge for labour markets and training policies in the context of rapid and substantial changes in skill needs. In most countries, a substantial share of employers complain that they cannot find workers with the skills that their businesses require. At the same time, many graduates face difficulties in finding job opportunities matching their qualifications.

In light of this challenge, OECD has undertaken an ambitious programme of work on how to achieve a better alignment of skill supply and skill demand, with a focus on: i) understanding how countries collect and use information on skill needs; ii) investigating cost-effective training and labour market policies to tackle skill mismatch and shortages; iii) studying the incentives of training providers and participants to respond to changing skill needs; and iv) setting up a database of skill needs indicators.

This work builds on the extensive programme of work of the OECD in the area of skills, including the OECD Skill Strategy and its follow up national implementation strategies, the Survey of Adult Skills (PIAAC) and its rich analyses in the areas of skills mismatch, vocational education and training and work-based learning.

The present report identifies effective strategies to tackle skills imbalances, based on five country-specific policy reports covering France, Italy, Spain, South Africa and the United Kingdom. It provides a comparative assessment of practices and policies in the following areas: the collection and use of information on skill needs to foster a better alignment of skills acquisitions with labour market needs; the design of education and training systems and their responsiveness to changing skill needs; the re-training of unemployed individuals; and the improvement of skills use and skills matching in the labour market. The assessment is based on country visits, in-depth research and data analysis conducted by the OECD secretariat in the five countries reviewed. Examples of good practice from other countries are also discussed.

The work on this report was carried out by Katharine Mullock and Glenda Quintini from the Skills and Employability Division of the Directorate for Employment, Labour and Social Affairs, under the supervision of Glenda Quintini (team manager on skills) and Mark Keese (Head of the Skills and Employability Division). The report draws on country-specific studies carried out by Fabio Manca, Katharine Mullock and Marieke Vandeweyer and has benefited from helpful comments provided by Stefano Scarpetta (Director for Employment, Labour and Social Affairs).

This report is published under the responsibility of the Secretary-General of the OECD, with the financial assistance of the JP Morgan Chase Foundation. The views expressed in this report should not be taken to reflect the official position of the JP Morgan Chase Foundation.

Table of contents

Figures

Table

Executive summary

Changing skill demands brought about by broad-based trends like globalisation, technological change and rapid population ageing have contributed to skill imbalances across OECD countries. Many employers report difficulties finding workers with the skills they require, and a high share of adults are working in jobs that are not well matched to their qualifications. While some degree of mismatch between the supply and demand for skills is inevitable, the cost of persistent skill imbalances for individuals, employers and society is substantial. Skill imbalances can lead to lower earnings and job satisfaction for workers, stunted productivity, and reduced economic growth. In light of these costs, the present report explores the role that policy can play in bringing about a better match between skill supply and skill demand, based on five country-specific policy reports covering France, Italy, Spain, South Africa and the United Kingdom (see OECD, 2017a, b, c, d and e, forthcoming).

All five of these countries have experienced significant labour market polarisation, that is to say, rising demand for high-level skills has been accompanied by a smaller increase in the employment share of low-skilled jobs, while employment shares for middle-skilled jobs have declined. Knowledge-intensive services have grown to represent a sizeable part of GDP in all four European countries. Similar polarisation trends have affected the South African economy which, however, continues to be characterised by a large primary sector. A remarkable convergence is found in the skills that are in shortage and surplus across the five countries. Skill shortages emerge primarily in social and creative skills as well as in science, technology, engineering, or mathematics (STEM) knowledge, while surpluses appear predominantly in routine non-cognitive skills.

Labour market indicators point to large pools of unused skills in France, Italy, Spain and South Africa. Unemployment is particularly high among those with no qualifications but, many tertiary graduates are also unemployed or in jobs that underutilise their skills. Poor employment outcomes of jobseekers and recent graduates can be linked to a weak match between their skills and those required in the labour market. All countries reviewed have a sizeable share of adults who lack basic literacy and numeracy skills and not enough tertiary graduates in France, Italy and Spain choose STEM degrees despite rising demand for these qualifications. Enrolment in vocational education is also low, generating shortages in many trade professions.

Besides a diagnosis of skill imbalances, this report provides a comparative assessment of practices and policies in place in the five countries reviewed to reduce skill imbalances. The assessment focuses on: the collection and use of skill needs information; education and training polices; policies to activate the unemployed; migration policies to attract and retain people with sought-after skills; and finally, policies to boost demand for higher-level skills.

Based on the five country reviews, and the detailed country-specific recommendations that were put forward, a set of best practice principles to guide the design of policies to reduce skill imbalances can be identified as follows:

- *Expand opportunities to participate in adult learning.* To adapt to changing skill demands, adults need better opportunities to upskill and retrain. Rising participation in non-standard working arrangements creates the need for learning incentives which are not directly tied to one's job. For example, France grants training leave rights to individuals which are preserved upon job loss and transferable between employers.

- *Link training for the unemployed to labour market needs.* Training programmes for the unemployed yield the most successful employment outcomes when they are tied closely to the needs of the labour market. One way to ensure that this happens is to focus public spending on training programmes for the unemployed on activities that address identified skill needs. For example, in Finland, public procurement of training courses for the unemployed is based on estimated regional labour market needs. Alternatively, as in France, governments can provide subsidies to employers to hire and train the unemployed, which aligns training with employers' needs.

- *Recognise informal and non-formal learning.* Validating informal and non-formal learning strengthens individuals' incentives to invest in training, helps to promote job-to-job transitions, and can reduce the incidence of under-qualification. In South Africa, recognition of prior learning has strengthened the signalling power of skills for individuals who had been previously denied access to quality formal education under the apartheid system.

- *Strengthen incentives for employers to invest in training to meet skill needs, but minimise the administrative burden.* Efforts to encourage employer investment in training need to steer training towards in-demand skills, while avoiding burdensome administrative processes which can reduce take-up. Small and medium-sized enterprises (SMEs) may be more likely to provide training if they receive assistance in developing training plans. For example, in Spain, a pilot initiative provides free technical support to SMEs interested in developing an apprenticeship programme, offering advice on which roles could be filled by an apprentice, and matching available vocational qualifications with the firm's skill needs.

- *Involve the social partners in vocational education.* Vocational education and work-based learning programmes can deliver skills needed by the labour market, especially where there is strong employer and trade union involvement. For example, in England under the new apprenticeship system, panels of employers (*trailblazers*) will take the lead in setting the curriculum requirements of apprenticeships.

- *Ensure higher and further education provision is responsive to skill needs in the labour market.* To reduce the misalignment between skills that are needed by employers and those that individuals acquire, governments can use funding arrangements for education and training institutions to steer the mix of provision in favour of subjects where there is high labour market demand. For instance, the Higher Education Funding Council of England (HEFCE) distributes public funds to higher education institutions in a way that promotes policy objectives, like the development of facilities related to STEM training (STEM Capital Fund).

- *Facilitate labour mobility, including the inflow of migrants with skills in high demand.* Enabling labour mobility within a country can reduce skill imbalances, as can the entry of foreigners with skills and qualifications which are in high demand. For instance, South Africa's *Critical Skills Visa* allows entry of foreigners who are qualified in skills on the country's Critical Skills List, even if they do not yet have a job offer.

- *Stimulate demand for higher-level skills.* Policies aimed at boosting the demand for higher-level skills can reduce over-qualification, while also contributing to higher productivity, growth and better job quality and well-being. For example, Italy's *Industria 4.0* proposes to shift the Italian productive system towards greater use of higher value-added technologies, which should stimulate demand for higher-level skills.

- *Ensure all relevant stakeholders are involved in the production of information on skill needs.* Co-ordination mechanisms can help to ensure that stakeholders work effectively together to assess and use skill needs information. Previously, the UK Commission for Employment and Skills played a key co-ordination role in the production of skills intelligence and in fostering responses at the sectoral and regional levels through the Sector Skill Councils.

- *Engage in regular monitoring and evaluation.* Rigorous evaluation of training programmes helps to improve their design by clarifying what works, what does not work, and under what conditions and for whom. Building monitoring and evaluation into the design and implementation of training programmes will help to ensure that scarce public resources are used efficiently and effectively.

References

OECD (2017a, forthcoming), *Getting Skills Right: Italy*, OECD Publishing, Paris.

OECD (2017b, forthcoming), *Getting Skills Right: South Africa*, OECD Publishing, Paris.

OECD (2017c, forthcoming), *Getting Skills Right: France*, OECD Publishing, Paris.

OECD (2017d, forthcoming), *Getting Skills Right: Spain*, OECD Publishing, Paris.

OECD (2017e, forthcoming), *Getting Skills Right: United Kingdom*, OECD Publishing, Paris.

Chapter 1

Drivers of skills demand and supply

The supply of and demand for skills are shaped by both structural and cyclical factors, each affecting the five countries being studied in different ways. For instance, economic growth, changes in the composition of economic output over time and the so-called mega-trends are all important macroeconomic factors influencing the demand for skills. On the other hand, labour market trends, migration and skills and education outcomes play an important role in defining the supply of skills. These factors are briefly considered in this chapter, highlighting similarities and differences across countries.

Changes in skill requirements as a result of the megatrends

The so-called megatrends – globalisation, technological progress and demographic change – are having a profound impact on the world of work. On the one hand, these "mega-trends" offer unparalleled opportunities for the creation of new and more productive jobs. On the other hand, technological progress, demographic change and globalisation will affect the skills that are required to enter and thrive in the labour market and put additional pressures on policy makers to provide individuals with opportunities to maintain their skills, upskill and/or reskill throughout their working lives.

Technological advances are allowing an increasing number of tasks traditionally performed by humans to become automated. Such automation used to focus primarily on routine tasks (e.g. clerical work, bookkeeping, basic paralegal work and reporting). However, with the advent of Big Data, artificial intelligence, the Internet of Things and ever-increasing computing power (i.e. the digital revolution), non-routine tasks are also increasingly likely to become automated. Technological advances are also allowing jobs to be de-bundled into a set of smaller tasks, some of which can be offshored to exploit comparative advantage resulting in a change in the skill content of jobs.

Figure 1.1.   ICT has spread fast in all four European countries

ICT capital services per hour worked, index (1995 = 100), 1995 to 2014

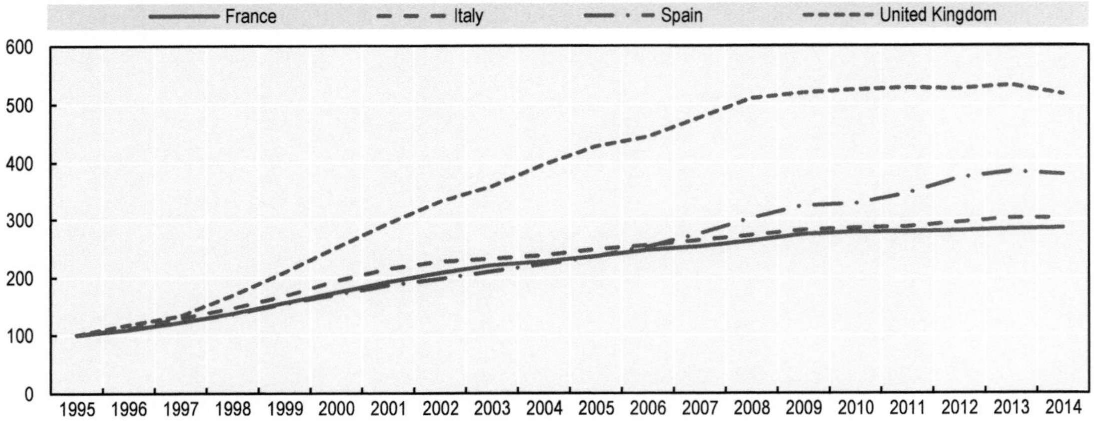

Note: ICT capital intensity per hours worked refer to the CAPIT_QPH variable in the EU KLEMS database. Data for Canada are taken from the World KLEMS database. Data series were extended using growth of the numerator and denominator of the ICT intensity ratio using the various releases of the EU KLEMS database (2009, 2013, and 2016). The 2009 EU KLEMS release covers the largest number of countries, covering the period from 1995 to 2007. Additional data was taken from later releases of EU KLEMS for the following countries: Austria, Belgium, Finland, France, Germany, Italy, the Netherlands, Spain and the United Kingdom. Values for Denmark have been adjusted to account for abnormally large increases in ICT intensity within the mining industry.

Source: EU KLEMS growth and productivity accounts, World KLEMS.

Demographic changes are also putting additional stress on policies to avoid skills obsolescence and tackle skill shortages. Over the next few decades, countries with ageing populations will undergo dramatic changes in the skill composition of their workforce. Shortages of qualified labour are likely to arise as large cohorts of older workers retire – increasing the need for health and care-related services, while also tightening the supply of labour. These shortages will coincide with increased pressure on adult learning systems to ensure that workers reskill and upskill as necessary to remain active for longer. On the other hand, in countries like South Africa (OECD, 2017b, forthcoming), youth represent a large part of the working-age population. While across OECD countries youth (15-24) only represent 20% of the working-age population (15-64), this share amounts to 31% in South Africa. The large share of youth in the labour market reflects one of South Africa's key advantages: a large and growing working-age population which promises substantial growth potential provided it can be employed productively. Policy makers in South Africa will have to ensure that youth have the skills necessary to enter the labour market and climb the career ladder, in order to harness the full potential of this demographic dividend.

Figure 1.2. Demographic challenges differ dramatically across countries

Estimated population growth, index (2015 = 1), 2015-50

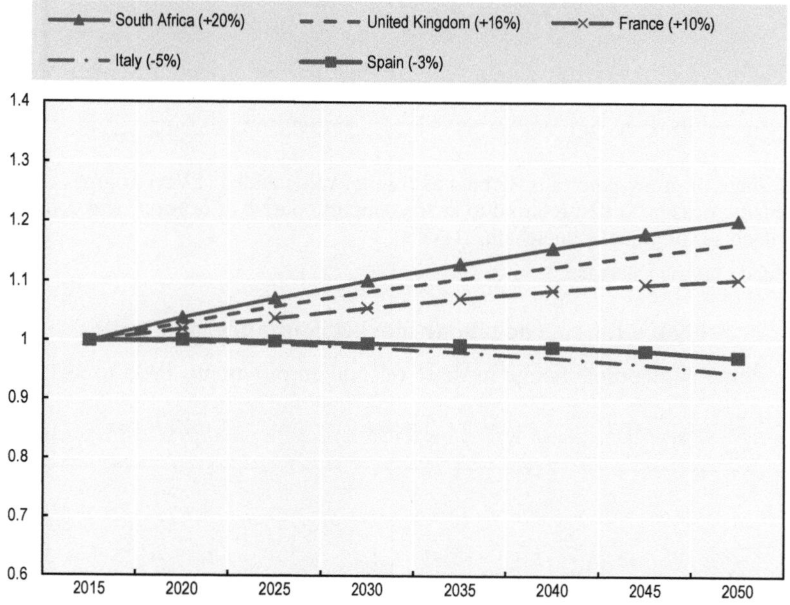

Source: United Nations World Population Prospects, the 2015 Revision.

Finally, *the world economy is becoming integrated through trade at an unprecedented pace*. The rapid fall in the cost of communication and transportation has not only promoted the integration of goods and services markets, but has also facilitated an accelerated pace of technological dissemination. These developments have been accompanied by innovations in business organisation which have allowed new trends in trade to develop, including the "trade in tasks" – global value chains, segmentation of production through offshoring, and global out-sourcing – all of which are allowing distant economies to be integrated into the global market.

The impact of the mega-trends on the overall number of jobs is uncertain: many jobs may disappear, but others are likely to be created elsewhere. What is certain is that labour markets across OECD countries will experience significant structural change, entailing significant reallocation of employment across sectors and occupations. This is likely to generate skills imbalances as countries adapt to the changes that are taking place. Tackling these imbalances is crucial for firms to harness the benefits brought about by the mega-trends by ensuring that they have access to a skilled and adaptable workforce. Addressing changing skill needs is also essential to shield workers from the negative effects of job loss and structural change.

Figure 1.3.   Increased linkages through global value chains, selected OECD countries, 1995 to 2011

Percentage point change in foreign value added share of gross exports, 1995 to 2011

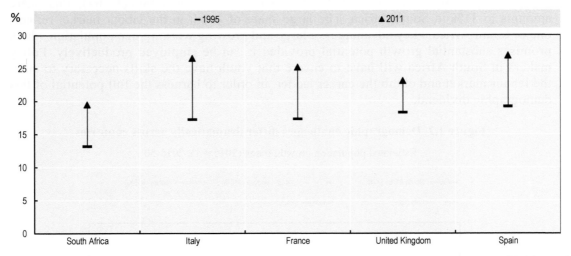

Note: Foreign value added share of gross exports is defined as foreign value added (FVA) in gross exports divided by total gross exports. It is an "FVA intensity measure" often referred to as the "import content of exports" and considered as a reliable measure of "backward linkages" in analyses of global value chains (GVCs).

Source: Trade in Value Added (TiVA) Database.

Figure 1.4.   The labour market continues to polarise

Percentage point change in share of total employment, 1995 to 2015

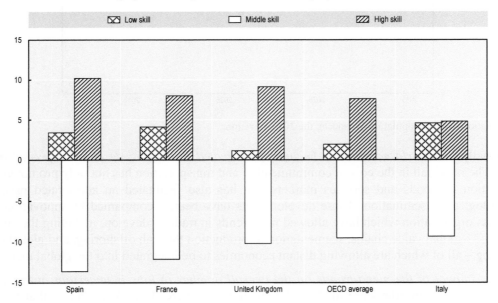

Note: High-skill occupations include jobs classified under the ISCO-88 major groups 1, 2, and 3. That is, legislators, senior officials, and managers (group 1), professionals (group 2), and technicians and associate professionals (group 3). Middle-skill occupations include jobs classified under the ISCO-88 major groups 4, 7, and 8. That is, clerks (group 4), craft and related trades workers (group 7), and plant and machine operators and assemblers (group 8). Low-skill occupations include jobs classified under the ISCO-88 major groups 5 and 9. That is, service workers and shop and market sales workers (group 5), and elementary occupations (group 9). The OECD average is a simple unweighted average of the 24 selected OECD countries analysed in Chapter 3 of the *OECD Employment Outlook 2017*.

Source: OECD (2017), *OECD Employment Outlook 2017*, OECD Publishing, Paris, http://dx.doi.org/10.1787/empl_outlook-2017-en.

Changes in the structure of output, employment and trade and polarisation in skills demand

Over the past decades, *all five countries have experienced a shift away from manufacturing towards service sector industries and jobs*. This trend has potentially important implications for the demand for skills. As in other OECD countries, in France, Italy, Spain and the United Kingdom, the importance of the manufacturing sector has declined strongly over the past few decades while the share of services in economic output has increased (OECD, 2017c, 2017d, 2017e, 2017f). Currently, manufacturing accounts for about 10% of value added in the United Kingdom, 11% in France, 15.5% in Italy and 13.2% in Spain. These figures compare with an EU average of 15.5%. On the other hand, services have grown in importance to represent the biggest share of value added, currently ranging between 78% in Italy and 85% in the United Kingdom.

Within these broad sectors of economic activity, the importance of knowledge-intensive services (ICT, financial and insurance and professional and scientific services) and high-tech manufacturing (pharmaceutical products, computer and electronic equipment and air and spacecraft machinery) can provide some indication of the demand of high-level skills. Knowledge-intensive services account for over 20% of value added in the United Kingdom, 17% in France, 15% in Italy and 12% in Spain, placing all countries above the EU28 average of 10%. High-tech manufacturing accounts for a much smaller share of value added, below the EU28 average of 2% for all four countries, mostly due to the declining share of the manufacturing sector overall. On the other hand, low-skilled services such as personal care and retail services have increased to account for about 20.5% of value added in Spain, 16% in France, Italy and the United Kingdom. Similarly, low-tech manufacturing still plays a significant role in Italy and Spain where it accounts for an above-average share of approximately 5.5%.[1]

Similar trends can be observed for South Africa, where the manufacturing sector has shrank to just 13.5% of GDP. However, the South African economy continues to be characterised by a large primary sector, including both agriculture and mining.

The recent global financial crisis has accentuated the process described above, with most job destruction between 2008 and 2011 taking place in manufacturing, construction and low-tech services and most job creation happening in knowledge-intensive services and public administration (Figure 1.5).

Figure 1.5. Where people lost their jobs: Job creation and destruction during the global financial crisis

Change in levels of employment as a percentage of the sum of absolute level changes, 2008-11

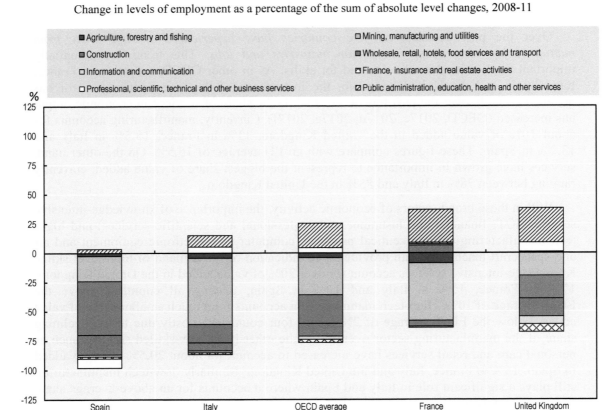

Source: OECD Structural Analysis (STAN) Database, ISIC Rev. 4, May 2013; *OECD National Accounts (SNA) Database* and national statistical institutes, June 2013.

Employment data paint a very similar picture: *the employment share of manufacturing has declined in all four countries since 1995 while the share of employment in services has increased.* Similarly to value added, the rise in service sector employment has happened primarily in knowledge-intensive services with low-tech services increasing slightly or remaining stable. However, knowledge-intensive service sector employment remains small ranging between 5.7% in Spain and 8.2% in the United Kingdom while the employment share of low-tech services attains 20-21% in the United Kingdom, France and Spain and 17% in Italy.

Figure 1.6. Employment in knowledge-intensive services, 2000-15

As a percentage of total employment

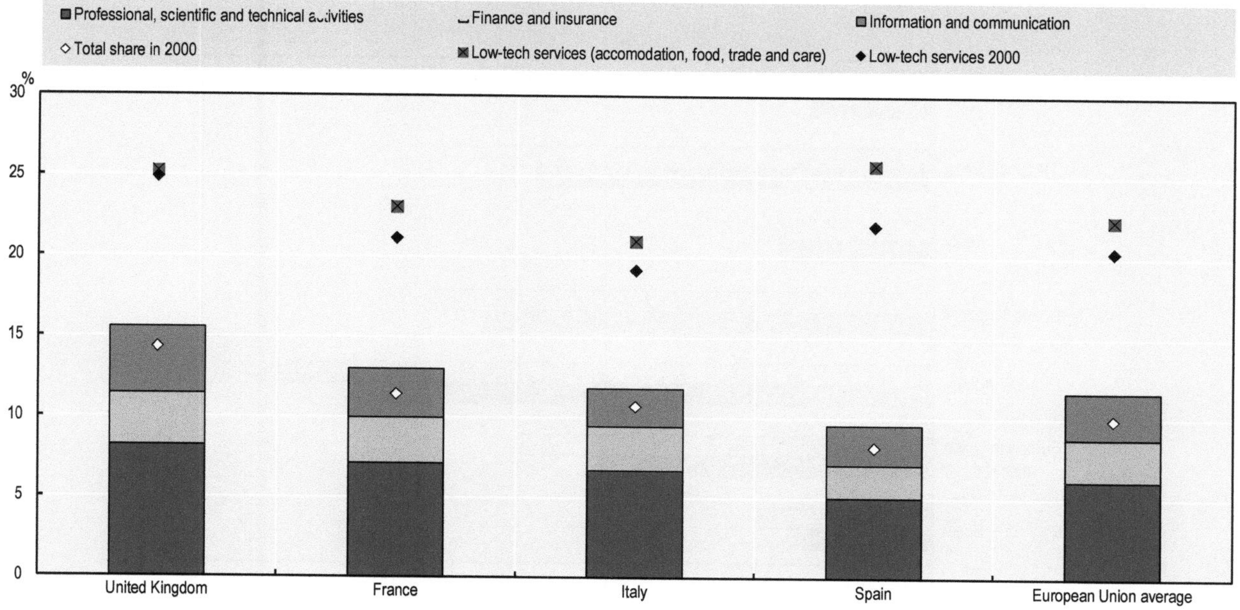

Source: OECD Structural Analysis (STAN) Database, ISIC Rev. 4, May 2013.

Finally, *export trends point to an increase in high-technology exports as a share of manufacturing exports.* As Figure 1.7 shows, 27% of manufacturing exports in France are in high-technology sectors and this is the case for 21% of UK manufacturing exports. Italy, Spain and South Africa, on the other hand, lag behind in terms of this indicator, with shares well below the EU average.

Merchandise trade dominates exports in all five countries but service exports have been rising in some. For instance, the share of services in UK exports has been rising and the country now exports a larger value of services than any other EU member state (both within the European Union and outside). Most of these services exports are in knowledge-intensive services: in 2010, the United Kingdom exported 18% of the world share of financial services, 8% of the world share of business services and 5% of the world share of ICT services, which together represented nearly 90% of all services exported from the United Kingdom (Department for Business Innovation and Skills, 2012). A similar trend has taken place in France, where the growth in service trade has now outpaced growth in goods trade. Service exports in France are dominated by "Other commercial services", representing 59% of "other business services". On the other hand, the manufacturing share of merchandise exports in South Africa is significantly smaller than in the EU28 as a result of South Africa's large mining sector, which represents 34.8% of exports. Compared to EU countries, South Africa also exports a relatively large share of agricultural products (12.5% compared to 7.9% in EU28). Service exports in South Africa are dominated by travel, whereas the largest share of service imports is transportation-related.

Figure 1.7. High-technology exports

Percentage of manufactured exports

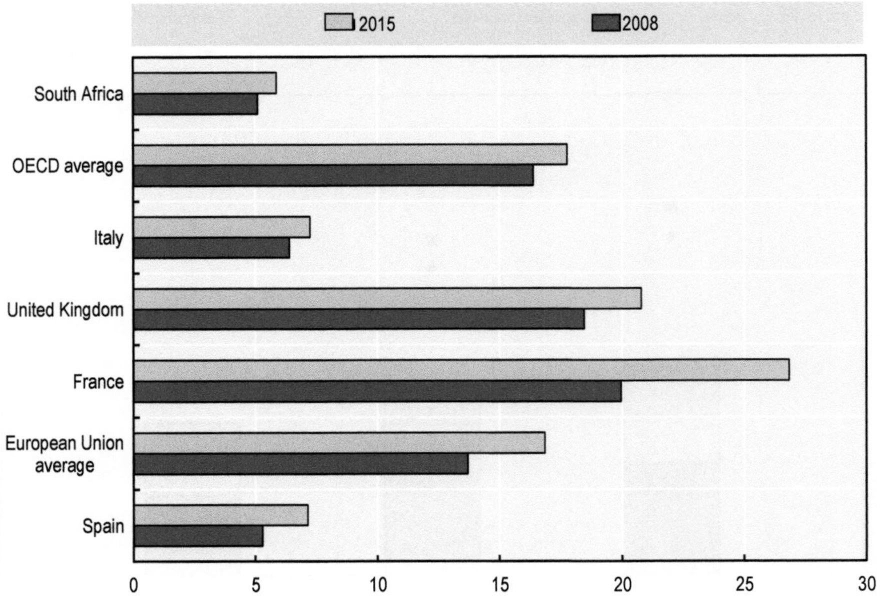

Source: World Bank, World Development Indicators, 2017.

Overall, in the four European countries examined, the picture emerging is one of polarised growth – in both high-tech and low-tech sectors – in line with the changes in employment portrayed in Figure 1.4 above. However, there are significant differences across countries. Output, trade and employment patters in France and the United Kingdom point more clearly to a rising demand for high-level skills. On the other hand, Spain and South Africa are geared towards more low-skilled employment. Finally, Italy stands somewhere in between with the various indicators painting a more mixed picture.

Science and innovation systems and skills demand

The analysis of innovation systems suggests sustained demand for high-level skills in France and the United Kingdom but less so in Italy, Spain and South Africa. Science and innovation indicators provide evidence of demand for higher-level skills. The picture emerging for the five countries is in line with that drawn above. France and, to a lesser extent, the United Kingdom have a relatively strong performance on science and innovation indicators, although they still fall far below the top-ranking countries like Switzerland and Sweden. Spain and Italy perform rather disappointingly; while South Africa performs close to the OECD bottom but above other emerging economies.

France scores above the OECD median for a range of science and innovation indicators (16 out of 22). The country is among the top performers for "patents filed by universities and public labs" and "fixed broadband subscriptions." France spends 2.26% of its GDP on R&D, which is more than the EU28 (1.95%) average and only slightly less than the OECD average (2.38%). Expenditure (expressed relative to GDP) has been growing steadily at about 1% on average per year during the period 2010-14, although the level of investment remains below the 2020 target set in the Europe 2020 framework (3% for France). The European Innovation Scoreboard confirms France's relatively strong performance, as its innovation index is 9% higher than the EU average (European Commission, 2016). Nonetheless, France innovation performance is significantly lower than the top-ranking countries for innovation (Switzerland, Sweden, Denmark and Finland).

The United Kingdom also performs above the OECD median for most indicators (14 out of 22) and excels in two of them: e-government and the share of doctoral graduates in science and engineering. On the other hand, public and private spending on R&D is significantly lower than France at just 1.7% of GDP.

As mentioned above, Italy and Spain's performance on science and innovation indicators are very similar and rather disappointing. Both countries spend far less than the OECD average on R&D – 1.27% for Italy and 1.22% for Spain – and score below the OECD median on almost all indicators. Only Italy is included in the top five performers in any one of the indicators, that of ease of entrepreneurship.

Finally, South Africa's performance on science and technology indicators is generally comparable with the bottom OECD countries. However, compared with other emerging economies (Argentina, Brazil, China, Colombia, India, Indonesia and the Russian Federation), the performance of South Africa in terms of science and innovation is relatively good. For half of the indicators, the South African performance is above the average for emerging economies, and the South African score is even the highest among available emerging economies for top universities, publications in top journals, triadic patents and patents filed by universities and public labs. Only for tertiary-education expenditure is South Africa the lowest-performing emerging economy. Notably, only 5.9% of South Africa's manufactured exports have high R&D intensity (UN Comtrade Database). This is very low compared to countries with similar income levels (20.6% in upper middle income countries). Compared with OECD countries, gross domestic expenditure on R&D as a proportion of GDP in South Africa is low (0.7% in 2011). While R&D expenditure expressed relative to GDP was on the rise in the period 2007-11 in OECD countries, it fell in South Africa (OECD, 2016a).

Table 1.1. Comparative performance of national science and innovation systems, selected OECD countries and South Africa, 2014

Country relative position: in the top five OECD or above (★), in the middle range on par or above OECD median (▲), in the middle range below OECD median (△) and in the bottom five OECD or below (○)

	Competences and capacity to innovate									
	Universities and public research			R&D and innovation in firms				Innovative entrepreneurship		
	Public R&D expenditure (per GDP)	Top 500 universities (per GDP)	Publications in the top-quartile journals (per GDP)	Business R&D expenditure (per GDP)	Top 500 corporate R&D investors (per GDP)	Triadic patent families (per GDP)	Trademarks (per GDP)	Venture capital (per GDP)	Young patenting firms (per GDP)	Ease of entrepreneur-ship index
	(a)	(b)	(c)	(d)	(e)	(f)	(g)	(h)	(i)	(j)
Denmark	★	★	★	▲	★	▲	▲	△		▲
Finland	★	★	▲	★	▲	▲	▲	▲	★	▲
France	▲	△	△	▲	▲	▲	▲	▲	△	▲
Italy	△	▲	△	△	△	△	△	○	▲	★
South Africa	○	△	○	○	△	○	△	▲		○
Spain	△	△	△	△	△	△	△	△	○	○
Sweden	★	★	★	▲	▲	▲	▲	★	★	△
Switzerland	★	▲	★	▲	★	★	★	▲	★	▲
United Kingdom	△	▲	▲	△	▲	▲	▲		△	▲

	Interaction and skills for innovation												
	ICT and internet infrastructures				Networks, clusters and transfers				Skills for innovation				
	ICT investment (per GDP)	Fixed broadband subscribers (per population)	Wireless broadband subscribers (per population)	E-government readiness index	Industry financed public R&D expenditure (per GDP)	Patents filed by universities and public labs (per GDP)	International co-authorship (%)	International co-invention (%)	Tertiary education expenditure (per GDP)	Adult population at tertiary education level (%)	Top adult performers in technology problem solving (%)	Top 15 year-old performers in science (%)	Doctoral graduate rate in science and engineering (%)
	(k)	(l)	(m)	(n)	(o)	(p)	(q)	(r)	(s)	(t)	(u)	(v)	(w)
Denmark	▲	★	▲	▲	△	▲	▲	△	▲	△	▲	△	▲
Finland	△	▲	★	▲	▲	▲	▲	△	▲	▲	★	★	★
France	▲	★	△	★	△	★	△	△	△	△		▲	▲
Italy	△	△	△	△	△	▲	△	○	○	○		△	△
South Africa	○	○	○	○	△	△	△	△	○	○			○
Spain	△	△	▲	▲	△	△	△	△	△	▲		△	△
Sweden	★	▲	★	▲	▲	△	▲	▲	▲	▲	★	△	★
Switzerland	★	★	★	▲	★	▲	★	▲	△	▲	▲	▲	★
United Kingdom	△	▲	▲	▲	△	▲	△	△	★	▲	▲	▲	★

Note: The chart shows the highest performing country along with the reviewed countries.

Source: OECD (2014), *OECD Science Technology and Industry Outlook 2014*, Table 9.1.

Labour market indicators of skills supply and demand

Labour market trends reflect both the demand for and supply of skills in the economy. Labour force participation is a clear indicator of skills supply. On the other hand, the number of unemployed individuals in the labour force is both a reflection of labour demand and an indication of the pool of available candidates for hiring firms. Finally, the nature of jobs – notably, type of contract and working hours – affect skills supply, particularly through the availability (or not) of training opportunities.

Labour market indicators point to large pools of unused skills in France, Italy, Spain and South Africa. In 2016, the labour force participation rate varied between 59% in South Africa to 77% in the United Kingdom (Figure 1.8). The differences across countries reflect sharp differences in the rate of participation of women which ranges from just 55% or less in Italy and South Africa to 67% and above in the other three countries. Similar gender disparities are observed when looking at employment rates. In addition, the low participation rate can be linked to high numbers of discouraged workers, i.e. persons who wanted to work but did not try to find work or start a business because they believed that there were no jobs available in their area, or were unable to find jobs requiring their skills, or they had lost hope of finding any kind of work. The share of discouraged workers reached 6.5% in South Africa in 2015 (Statistics South Africa, 2016), compared to only 0.5% across OECD countries in 2013.

Cross-country differences in unemployment rates, overall and for young people, are even more striking. This reflects different GDP growth rates in the countries examined but also institutional differences affecting structural unemployment rates. In 2016, the unemployment rate of 15-64-year-old adults was lowest in the United Kingdom, where it stood at just 5%. This compared with rates of 10% in France, 12% in Italy, 20% in Spain and a staggering 27% in South Africa. With the exception of the United Kingdom, these rates put all countries above the relevant OECD average. In contrast to France, Italy and Spain, South Africa's high unemployment rate is not just a recent phenomenon related to the recent global financial crisis: it has fluctuated around 25% during the last 25 years, with only a short period of lower unemployment in the mid-nineties. While unemployment was on the decline in the years before the start of the global financial crisis, it has been on the rise ever since.

Young people in France, Italy, Spain and South Africa have a high probability of being unemployed. In 2016, 13% of persons aged 15-24 were unemployed in the United Kingdom, in line with the OECD average but well below the rate in France (24.6%), Italy (37.8%), Spain (44.5%) and South Africa (53.3%). With the exception of the United Kingdom, the rate remained significantly above its pre-crisis level in all countries. These mass youth unemployment rates point to a large pool of unutilised skills that hiring employers can choose from, reducing somewhat the likelihood of skill shortages. However, unemployed youth may not possess the skills required to enter the labour market, making the co-existence of high unemployment rates and skill shortages possible.

The poor labour market situation of youth in France, Italy and Spain is also reflected in the relatively high share of youth not in employment, education or training (NEET). The share of NEET youth in 2014 reached 23% in France, 30% in Italy and 35% in Spain, all substantially higher than the OECD average of 20%. Although this group of inactive and unemployed youth who are not in education is mostly made up of school drop-outs – youth who have left education without an upper secondary certificate or qualification – a sizeable share has completed tertiary education (see Figure 1.9). The most educated among NEETs tend to be unemployed or inactive young females, hence they represent a group relatively close to the labour market if given the opportunity or supported through childcare policies.

While a comparable disaggregation of NEET rates is not available for South Africa, the overall NEET rate in South Africa was 36% among persons aged 15-29 in 2015, compared with an OECD average for this age group of 14.6% (OECD, 2016a). The share increases to over 50% when focusing on 22-24 year-olds. South African woman are 5.4 percentage points more likely to be NEET than men (Statistics South Africa, 2016). Focusing on the group of 20-24 year-olds, the NEET rate decreases substantially with educational attainment, ranging from 74% among people without any schooling to 44.7% for people with upper secondary education (grade 12, also referred to as Matric in South Africa). Ensuring good labour market outcomes for youth is especially important in South Africa, where youth represent a very large part of the working-age population.

Figure 1.8. Key labour market performance indicators in 2016: Total, women, youth

Panel A. Total labour force participation rate and female labour force participation rate, 2016

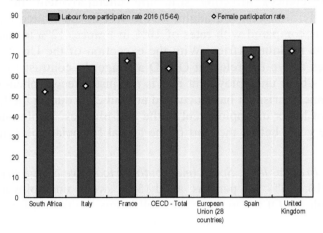

Panel B. Total unemployment rate and youth unemployment rate, 2016

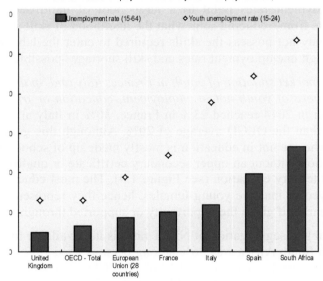

Panel C. Employment rate (total, women and youth), 2016

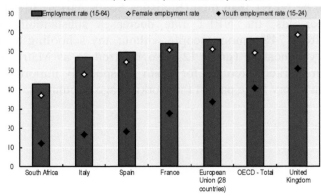

Note: The chart shows OECD and EU averages along with the reviewed countries.

Source: OECD Labour Market Database.

Figure 1.9. Youth neither in employment nor in education or training, by educational attainment, 2013-14

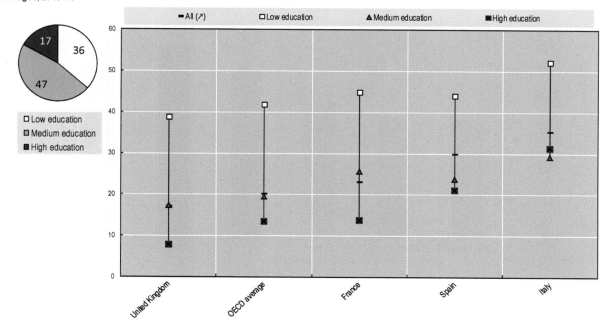

Note: Data in Panel B refer to 2014. "Low-education" denotes lower-secondary school and lower (Levels 0-2 in the International Standard Classification of Education [ISCED]); "medium education" refers to upper- or post-secondary education (ISCED Levels 3-4); and "high education" means higher, or tertiary, education (ISCED Levels 5-6).

Source: OECD calculations based on the European Labour Force Survey and national labour force surveys.

Not only does unemployment represent a pool of unused skills but it also poses a risk of skill depreciation and obsolescence if it persists over time. In Italy, Spain and South Africa more than half of the unemployed have been looking for work for longer than one year – they are long-term unemployed. This share is lower but still very high in France (40%) while it stands at 36% in the United Kingdom, very close to the OECD average of 35%. Long spells of unemployment reduce employment prospects even when the economy starts to recover because skills become obsolete, the unemployed lose contact with professional networks, and employers may prefer to hire candidates with recent work experience (OECD, 2012).

Migrants represent another potential skill reservoir in the presence of skill shortages and their share in the overall population has been rising steadily in France, Italy, the United Kingdom and South Africa. This is not the case in Spain, where net migration flows have dropped to negative levels since the economic crisis which affected migrants very badly – particularly those working in the construction sector.

Figure 1.10. Long-term unemployment rate, 2013

Share of unemployed individuals

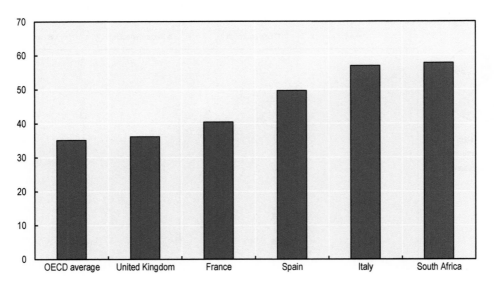

Note: Long-term unemployment is defined as unemployment lasting 12 months or more.

Source: OECD Labour Force Statistics.

Differences in labour market outcomes between foreign- and native-born individuals point to high underutilisation of the skills of migrants (Figure 1.11). In France, Italy and Spain, the unemployment rate of foreign-born individuals is significantly higher than that of the native-born and this difference is particularly large in France (10 percentage points) and Spain (11 percentage points). This is not the case in the United Kingdom and South Africa where the foreign-born population has comparable or better employment outcomes than the native-born population. In the United Kingdom this is the result of selective migration policies.[2] UK immigrants are younger and more educated than their UK-born counterparts, and this educational attainment gap has risen over time (Rienzo, 2016; Wadsworth, 2015). This translates into better labour market performance than the EU average for foreign-born populations. In 2014, working-age immigrants faced an unemployment rate of 7.1%, compared with 6.3% for the native-born, a gap of only 0.8 percentage points, which is low relative to the EU average gap of 4.5 percentage points. A similar picture emerges for South Africa where the foreign-born population has better labour market outcomes than the native born population (Fauvelle-Aymar, 2014). The unemployment rate of international migrants (14.7%) is lower than that of non-migrants (26.1%). Immigrants in South Africa are also less likely to be discouraged, as only 3.8% is considered to be a discouraged jobseeker, compared to 8.4% of non-migrants and 6.8% of domestic migrants. However, international migrants in South Africa are much more likely to be employed in the informal sector (32.7% compared to 16.6% for non-migrants), and over half of those who are employed are in precarious jobs (53.29% compared to 30.3% of non-migrants).

Heightening the skills utilisation problem, in France, Italy and the United Kingdom, differences in labour market outcomes are larger for highly-educated immigrants than for low-educated immigrants. In the United Kingdom, highly-educated immigrants face unemployment rates that are 2.7 percentage points higher than their native-born counterparts, while low-educated immigrants face nearly identical unemployment rates to their native-born counterparts (15.0% vs. 14.3%) (OECD, 2015a). Similarly, in France, the underutilisation of migrant skills is more prominent among the high-skilled foreign-born population: the employment rate gap for 25-64 year-olds is larger for middle and high-skilled individuals (12.8 and 13.9 percentage points, respectively) than for the low-skilled population (5.6 percentage points). These differences are likely to be related to difficulties in the recognition of the skills acquired outside the country. On the other hand, few highly-educated immigrants are drawn to Spain and Italy for employment. In Spain, most immigrants work in the services sector, and particularly in the lowest-skill jobs ("elementary occupations"), which largely comprise domestic help and agricultural labourers (Observatorio de las Ocupaciones, 2015). Immigrants working in the Spanish construction sector represented 17.5% of all immigrant contracts in 2008, but by 2014 they represented only 6.3% (Observatorio de las Ocupaciones, 2015). On the other hand, international migrants in South Africa fare better in the labour market than native South-Africans, even when controlling for differences in education.

Finally, in South Africa, Spain and Italy, high-skilled emigration has been growing fast and could represent a drag to innovation and research and development. The United Kingdom is a receiving countries of much of this emigration, thanks to its better labour market performance and highly-ranked tertiary education institutions. For instance, the United Kingdom attracts an impressive 12.6% of the worldwide market share of international tertiary-level students, second only to the United States (16.4%). The United Kingdom's share of the global market has grown more than any other country since 2000, suggesting its tertiary educational system presents a strong draw for foreign talent (OECD, 2015). What is more, many of those moving to study at a UK university remain in the country after graduation, contributing to the large pool of highly-skilled migrants mentioned above. Other countries perform less well. The Global Talent Competitiveness Index (GTCI) 2017 provides an in-depth analysis of how countries are competing globally to grow better talent, attract the talent they need and retain those workers who contribute to competitiveness, innovation, and growth of each country. While the GCTI places the United Kingdom in the third position globally (Switzerland and Singapore are in first and third), France, Spain and Italy are, instead, in positions 24, 35 and 40 of the ranking respectively. South Africa is instead, in the 64th position of the 118 countries examined.

Figure 1.11. Unemployment rate of foreign-born and native-born populations, 2015

Unemployment rate, 15-64 (%)

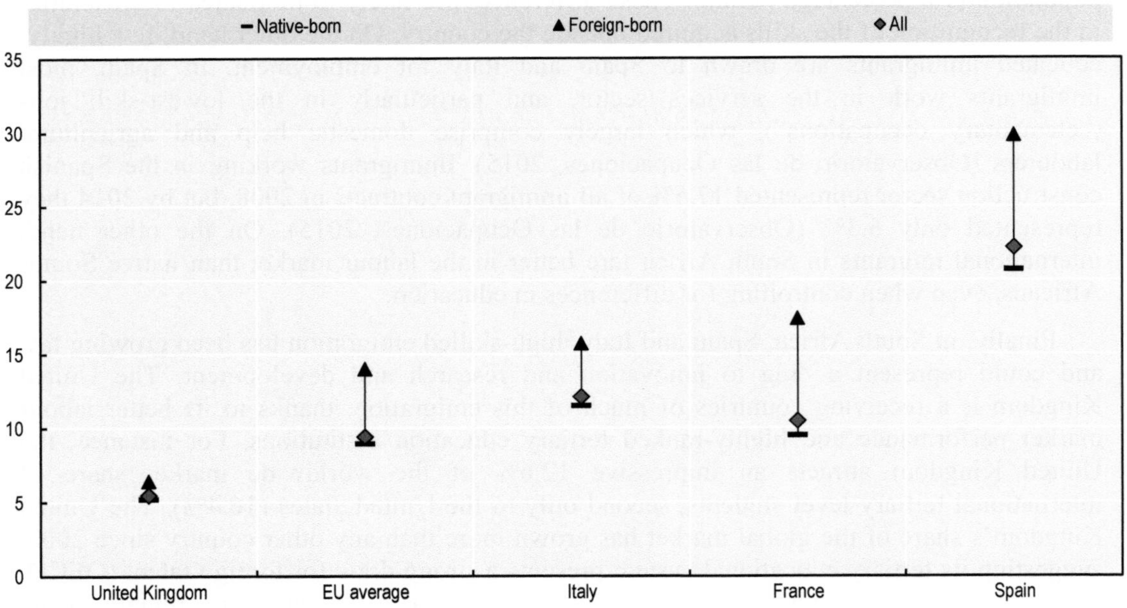

— Native-born   ▲ Foreign-born   ◆ All

	United Kingdom	EU average	Italy	France	Spain

Source: OECD Migration Statistics.

Skill use and development in the workplace

Skills are often not used to the full and nurtured in the workplace. Skills are not used to the same extent in all jobs and across countries. For instance, part-time and fixed-term jobs provide fewer opportunities for skills accumulation than full-time and permanent jobs, respectively. In addition, skills use is lower in these jobs all else being equal (OECD, 2016b).

Across countries and skill types, jobs in France, Italy and Spain tend to be characterised with skill use below the OECD average and far below Australia and New Zealand, the top performing countries in the use of most types of skills. This is the case for basic skills such as reading, writing and numeracy and for ICT skills. Differences in the use of problem solving at work are less dramatic with France and Spain very close to the OECD average and Italy close to the best performers. On the other hand, England performs rather well on all dimensions of skills use at work.

Large numbers of young people and female workers in France, Italy and Spain are employed in temporary or part-time jobs, respectively. However, these jobs provide limited opportunities for training and skill use. In Spain, 70% of young people are employed on temporary contracts and this rate is also alarmingly high in France (60%) and Italy (57%). In OECD countries temporary workers have a lower probability of accessing employer-sponsored training than permanent workers. This difference is extremely large in France (-27%) and Spain (-17%) while data for Italy is not available. French, Italian and Spanish temporary workers also have a lower probability of transitioning to permanent employment compared to most other OECD countries (OECD, 2014). Compared to workers with permanent contracts, temporary workers also have a higher probability of becoming unemployed. All these facts contribute to an increased likelihood of skills obsolescence and depreciation among workers on temporary contracts. On the other hand, the picture is rather different for the United Kingdom, where only 15% of working youth are employed on temporary contracts and there is no statistically significant difference in the likelihood of undergoing training between temporary and permanent jobs.

Figure 1.12. Skill use at work

Index of skill use at work based on task information

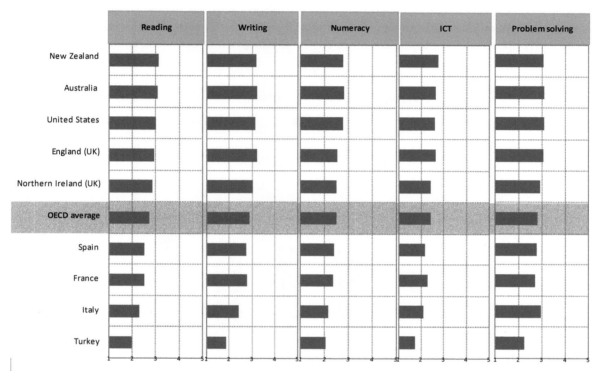

Note: The chart shows the highest and lowest performing countries, OECD average along with the available reviewed countries.

Source: Survey of Adult Skills (PIAAC) 2012, 2015.

A different picture emerges for part-time work which is more common in the United Kingdom than in the other four countries examined. Almost one in four UK workers are employed on a part-time basis – i.e. they work less than 30 hours per week – and this share increases to 37% among working women (Figure 1.13). Italy has the second highest incidence of female part-time employment at 32% while France and Spain rank far behind at 22% and 23%, respectively. While part-time work has the potential benefit of allowing a better work-life balance, particularly for women with young children, it is not always a choice. Involuntary part-time employment, whereby employees only work on a part-time basis because they cannot find a full-time job is widespread. For instance, in Spain, more than half of part-time employment is involuntary (63% against the OECD average of 17.4% in 2015). And these figures do not include those who would work full-time if adequate and affordable childcare facilities were available. Overall, high involuntary part-time employment could represent a pocket of unused skills at risk of depreciation and obsolescence.

In South Africa, non-standard work tends to take the form of informal work rather than part-time or temporary employment. Around 17% of employment in South Africa in 2015 was in the informal sector.[3] The probability of being employed in the informal sector is highest for black Africans and low-skilled (incomplete high school or below) workers (Statistics South Africa, 2015). The share of the informal sector is largest in the trade, construction and transport sectors, while it is negligible in the mining industry. In South Africa, however, many people work in precarious jobs even outside the informal sector. This is reflected in the share of employment in the "informal economy", which includes all persons working in the informal sector as well as those persons working in the formal sector who are not entitled to basic benefits or protection. The ILO estimates the informal economy in South Africa to represent around 33% of total employment. The relative size of the South African informal economy is comparable to China (32.6%), and is smaller than in most other upper-middle income countries (with the exception of European countries).

Figure 1.13. Incidence of part-time and temporary work: Total, female, youth

Panel A. Share of part-time workers in total employment, total (1995 and 2015) and all women (2015)

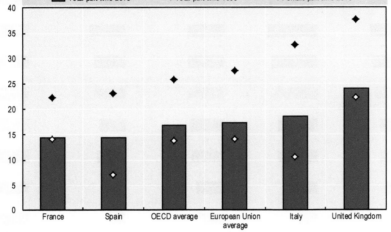

Panel B. Share of temporary workers in total employment, total (1995 and 2015) and youth (2015)

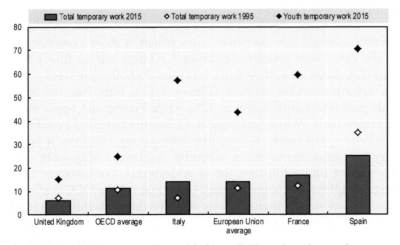

Note: The chart shows the OECD and EU averages along with the available reviewed countries.

Source: OECD Labour Force Statistics.

Educational attainment and skill levels

The labour market factors analysed above influence the pool of available labour but say little about the quality of the human capital available in each economy: educational attainment and skill levels can help to shed light on the latter aspect.

Educational attainment varies but the share of tertiary graduates has risen in all countries. Only in the United Kingdom is tertiary attainment higher than in the OECD on average. In 2015, 43.5% of UK citizens aged 25-64 had completed tertiary education, compared with only 36% across OECD countries (see Figure 1.14). In the same year, the share of adults with a tertiary qualification was slightly below the OECD average in France (34%) and Spain (35%) and was very low at just 18% in Italy. However, the United Kingdom also had a very large share of adults without an upper secondary qualification, close to 40% and comparable to that observed in Italy and Spain. This was not the case in France where only about one in five adults has not completed high-school. In terms of overall educational attainment, all four countries stood well below Canada – the top-performing country with 9% of adults holding no qualification, 35% holding an upper secondary diploma and 55% holding a tertiary degree.

In South Africa, educational attainment is on the rise but remains low compared with OECD countries (not shown in Figure 1.14). In 2014, 35% of the South Africans aged 25-64 had below upper secondary educational attainment, 56% had upper secondary and post-secondary non-tertiary educational attainment, and only 7% had tertiary educational attainment. While there has been a substantial shift from lower secondary education to upper secondary, the share of individuals with tertiary education has only increased modestly (from around 5% in the early 2000s). The share of individuals without any education dropped spectacularly from 12.3% in 2002 to 6.1% in 2014. The improvement in educational attainment in South Africa is also clear when focusing on the group of 25-34 year-olds, as almost three quarters of them have upper secondary or post-secondary non-tertiary educational attainment. The gap in educational attainment between men and women has now closed in all four OECD countries and almost closed in South Africa. In each of the European countries in this review, women are now better educated than their male counterparts which makes their lower participation in the labour market more problematic in terms of skills utilisation.

Figure 1.14. Educational attainment of the adult population, OECD countries, 2014

Percentage of population aged 25-64

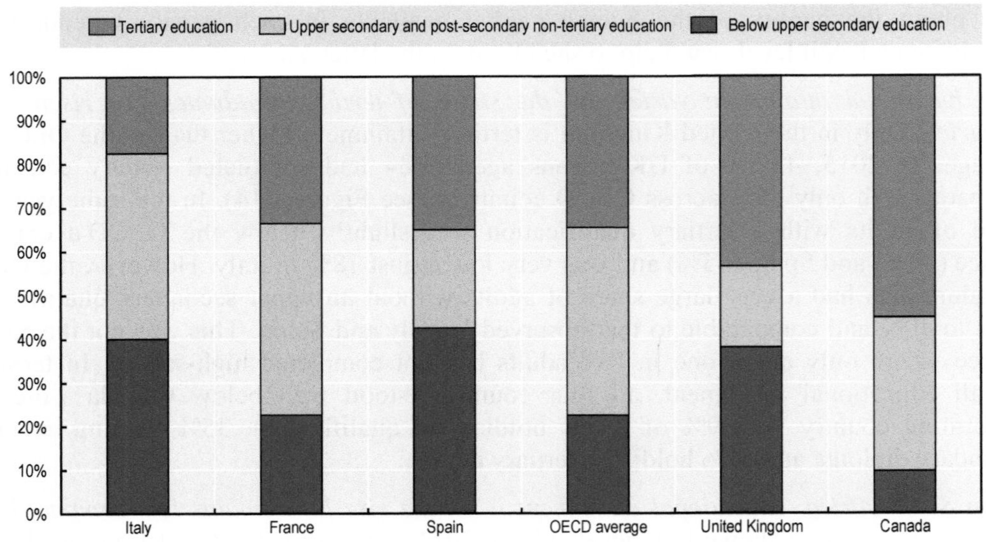

Note: Data refer to 2013 for France. The chart shows the highest performing country, the OECD average and the reviewed countries for which data is available.

Source: *OECD Education and Training Database.*

The share of STEM graduates is very high in the United Kingdom but lags behind in France, Italy and Spain. The value of tertiary degrees in the labour market – in terms of wages and employability – varies depending on the subject of graduation. As discussed above, technological change is likely to increase the demand for science, technology, engineering and mathematics (STEM) skills, giving graduates in these fields good employment opportunities. In addition, the share of STEM graduates influences the ability of firms to innovate and invest in R&D. However, countries vary in the share of students pursuing these subjects. In the United Kingdom, 16% per cent of tertiary students graduate in the field of sciences in the United Kingdom – which puts the United Kingdom at the top of the OECD country distribution for this indicator. In Spain and France this share is just about 9% and in Italy it is a mere 7%.

Figure 1.15. Share of STEM graduates, 2014

Share of tertiary graduates in science, mathematics and computing, 2014

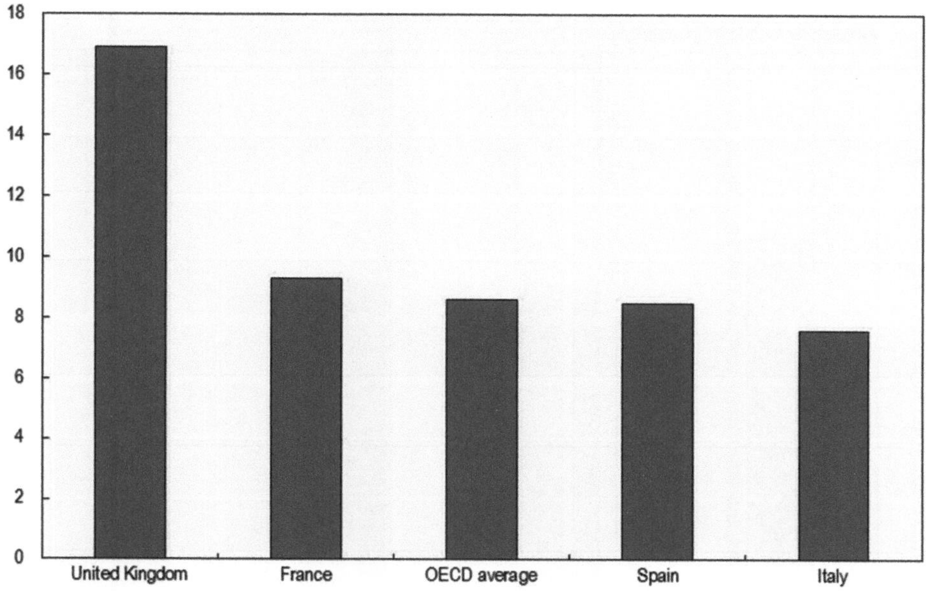

Source: OECD (2016), *Education at a Glance 2016: OECD Indicators,* OECD Publishing, Paris, http://dx.doi.org/10.187/eag-2016-en.

Enrolment in work-based vocational education lags behind the best performers in all countries. Vocational education and work-based learning programmes are often perceived as providing skills that are closer to those required in the labour market than general programmes. Among the countries examined, enrolment in vocational programmes is highest in Italy at about 60% of secondary students, followed by France, the United Kingdom and Spain (Figure 1.15). Besides enrolment rates, the quality of vocational education pathways is crucial and a key feature is the extent to which they involve a period of work-based practice. In the United Kingdom and France, work-based spells exist and account for about 10% and 25% of secondary enrolments, respectively. Spain introduced a work-based programme for vocational education in 2012, though participation is still low, with about 15 000 students having participated during the 2015/16 academic year.

Figure 1.16. Distribution of students enrolled in upper-secondary education, by programme orientation, 2014

Percentage of all upper secondary students

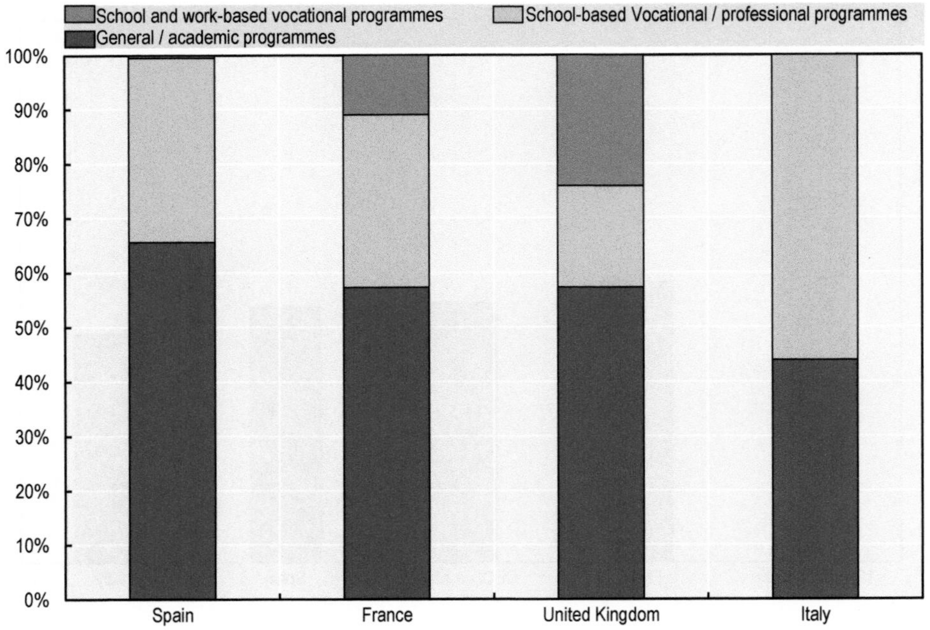

Note: When no separate data on school and work-based vocational programmes is available, the students from this category are included in the school-based programmes category.

Source: OECD (2016), *Education at a Glance 2016: OECD Indicators,* OECD Publishing, Paris, http://dx.doi.org/10.187/eag-2016-en.

Large shares of adults in France, Italy, Spain and South Africa have alarmingly low basic skills. International skills assessments provide an indication of the quality of education and training. Based on the OECD Survey of Adult Skills (PIAAC), and among the reviewed European countries, only English adults (age 16-65) score at or above average in literacy and numeracy, while adults in France, Italy and Spain score at the bottom of both scales. Even English adults, however, stand far behind their counterparts in the best performing countries, such as Finland and Japan. For instance, only one in two respondents in England scores at levels 3 to 5 in literacy compared with about 42% in France and about 30% in Italy and Spain. In Finland and Japan, this share exceeds 60%. The share of adults scoring at the lowest levels of literacy also influences the overall poor performance of the countries examined: fewer than 5% of adults score at level 1 or below in Japan but this shares attains 27% in Italy and Spain, 22% in France and 16% in England.

When focusing on young adults (16-24 year-olds), France, Italy and Spain rank much better, at or close to the OECD average. On the other hand, England is among a minority of countries where young people perform worse on literacy and numeracy than either prime-aged adults (25-54) or seniors (55-65). This decline in test scores from generation to generation could suggest deterioration in the quality of schooling over time (OECD, 2016d).

Figure 1.17. Literacy proficiency of adults (16-65)

Percentage of adults scoring at each proficiency level in literacy

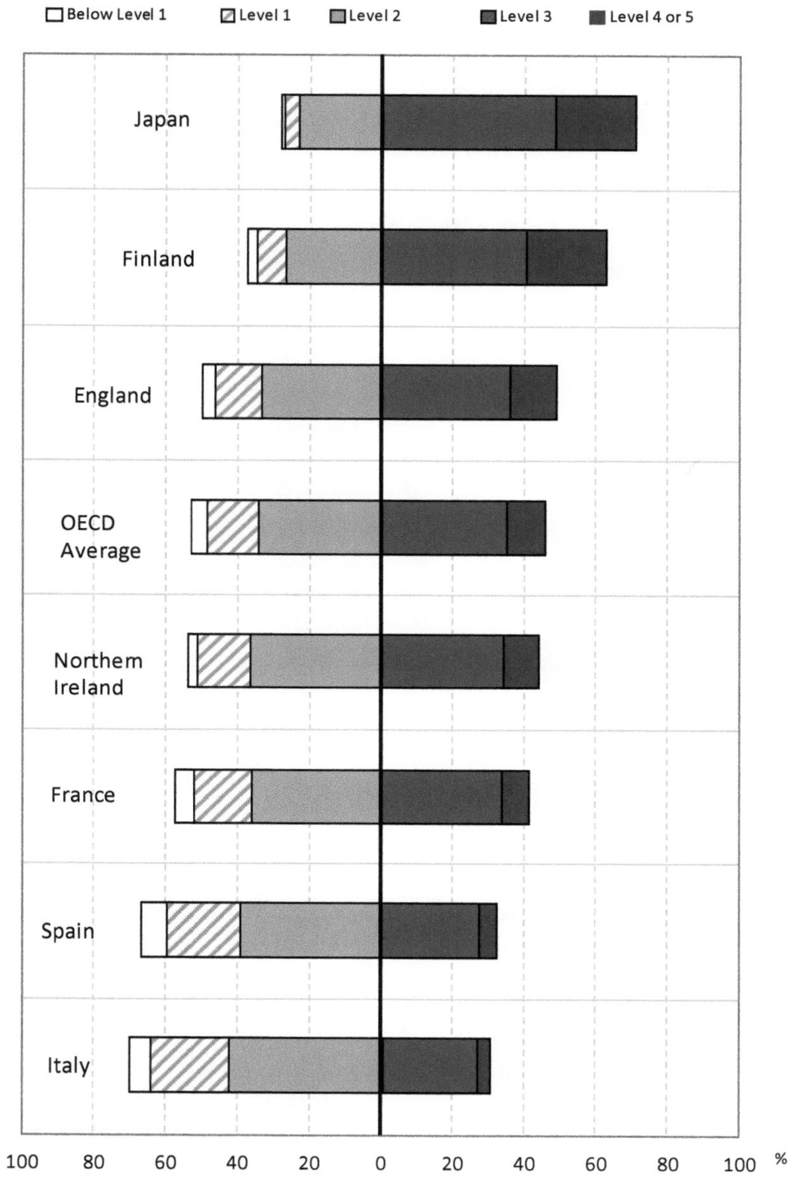

Source: Survey of Adult Skills (PIAAC) 2012, 2015.

PIAAC data is not available for South Africa but other data sources can be exploited to look at the skills of the country's population. The performance of South Africa in TIMSS, a survey measuring mathematics and science skills of eighth grade students (around 14 years old)[4] across a range of countries, gives an indication of the quality of the South African education system. In the last round of the TIMSS survey, South Africa ranked 38th out of 39 participating countries in mathematics and last in science (Mullis et al., 2016). Figure 1.18 shows that South Africa's average test score is low compared to participating OECD and upper-middle income countries.[5] Although South African students' skill level remained low in the 2015 evaluation, it had increased substantially compared to 2002 and 2011 (Department of Basic Education, 2013). Between 2002 and 2011 the greatest improvement was among the "most disadvantaged" learners, who scored the lowest initially (Reddy et al., 2012). However, big differences remained between students from different types of schools (public versus independent) and schools with different historical background.

Figure 1.18. Mathematics and science performance of eight graders, South Africa, Italy, England and selected upper-middle income countries, 2015

Average mathematics and science score (TIMSS)

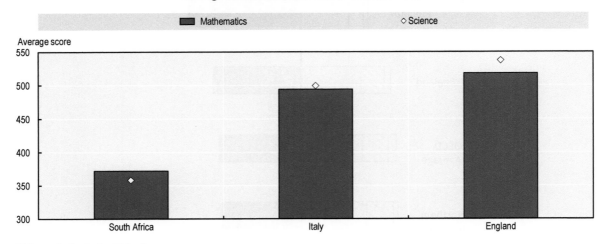

Note: China only includes Taipei.

Source: Mullis et al. (2016).

Tertiary graduates also perform poorly in basic skills, particularly in Spain and Italy. Tertiary education also plays a fundamental role in creating the supply of high-level skills that are much discussed in the context of the so-called "knowledge economy". Results from the OECD survey of Adults Skills (PIAAC), show that tertiary qualifications do not necessarily translate into higher basic skills. Tertiary graduates in Italy and Spain perform just about the same as upper secondary graduates in Japan or the Netherlands. Large differences can also be observed in terms of the gaps in average scores between tertiary and upper secondary graduates: this gap is very small in Italy, possibly explaining small wage premia for tertiary qualifications in the country; while it is very large in France.

Figure 1.19. Literacy proficiency score of adults, by educational attainment

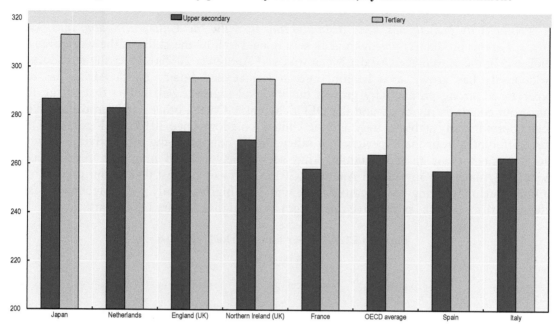

Note: The chart shows the highest performing country, OECD average along with the available reviewed countries.

Source: Survey of Adult Skills (PIAAC) 2012, 2015.

Adult learning opportunities are limited and tend to benefit higher-skilled adults most. Given that many working-age adults have low basic skills, opportunities to continue learning while working are particularly critical to equip workers with the necessary skills to benefit from globalisation and technological change. In England, about 50% of adults aged 25-64 participated in at least one job-related learning activity, in the year prior to the 2012 Survey of Adult Skills. This share was just 20% in Italy, 32% in France and 35% in Spain. Like in other countries, participation in learning activities is strongly correlated to skill proficiency, with higher-skilled adults more likely to take up training.

Figure 1.20. Participation in formal and non-formal adult education and training, total and low-skilled adults

Percentage of working-age population

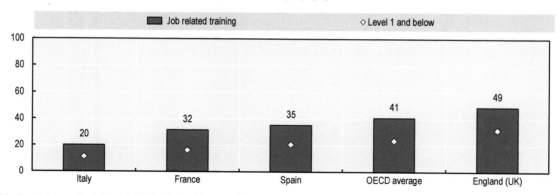

Note: This chart shows that low-skilled adults (those who score at Level 1 or below in PIAAC) have a lower probability of participating in adult education and training than the general population.

Source: Survey of Adult Skills (PIAAC) 2012, 2015.

Productivity developments

Productivity growth has been disappointing in Italy, the United Kingdom and South Africa. Labour productivity growth is closely related to how the skills of the workforce are allocated in the workplace (Adalet McGowan and Andrews, 2015a). Over the past decade, productivity has grown at a healthy rate in France and Spain. South Africa has also experienced strong productivity growth but its level remains well below that of the four European countries reviewed and the OECD average. On the other hand, productivity has been approximately stable in Italy and the United Kingdom since 2010 (see Figure 1.21). In fact, differently from the experience of other OECD countries, the productivity of Italy's most efficient firms in the manufacturing sector has declined in recent years. Recent evidence (Adalet McGowan and Andrews, 2015) seems to suggest that labour productivity in Italy's manufacturing sector could be around 20% higher if Italy's most technologically advanced firms were as productive (and large) as the global frontier benchmark.

Figure 1.21. GDP per hour worked, 2001-16

2010 USD PPP

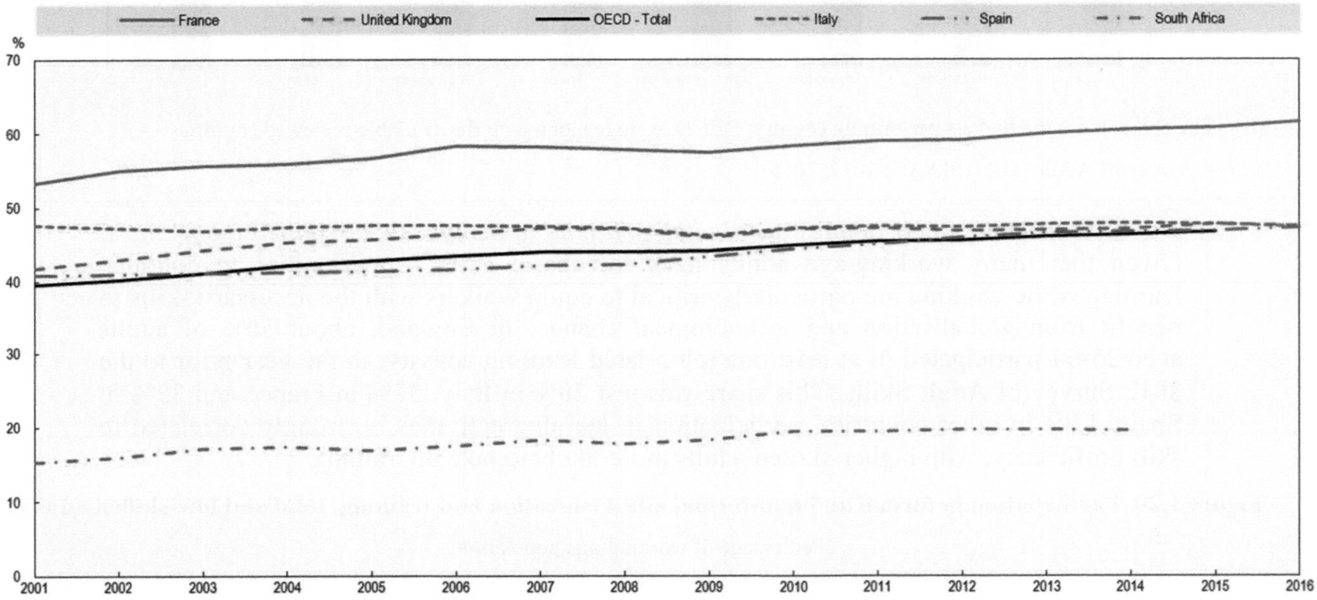

Source: OECD National Accounts Database, World Bank National Accounts Database.

Notes

1. These observations are strengthened by country-specific analysis. For the United Kingdom, BIS (2012) and Salvatori (2015) show that growth in services has taken place in both knowledge-intensive services like finance, business services, and information and communications technology (ICT), but also in lower-skill service sectors, like personal care and sales. Declines in manufacturing activity have led to a drop in employment in middle-skill occupations, particularly in craft occupations and plant and machine operatives (Salvatori, 2015). While growth in employment since the early 1980s was observed in both the highest-paid (top two deciles) and lowest-paid (bottom two deciles) occupations, most of employment growth took place in the highest-paid occupations (Green, 2016; Salvatori, 2015).

2. In the United Kingdom, labour migration consists of free movement of European Economic Area (EEA) citizens and restricted migration from outside the EEA via a points-based system that facilitates entry of skilled immigrants. Over the last few years, the goal of UK immigration policy has been to encourage immigration of skilled migrants while reducing overall immigration (Home Office, 2015).

3. The informal sector in South Africa is defined as i) employees working in establishments that employ fewer than five employees, who do not deduct income tax from their salaries/wages, and ii) employers, own-account workers and persons helping unpaid in their household business who are not registered for either income tax or value-added tax.

4. In South Africa, grade 9 students rather than grade 8 students participate to TIMSS. Their average age is 16.

5. In 2015 South Africa participated for the first time in the Grade 4 TIMSS assessment (for mathematics only). The results are similar to the 8-grade results, with South Africa ranking 48th among 49 participating countries.

References

Adalet McGowan, M. and D. Andrews (2015a), "Labour Market Mismatch and Labour Productivity: Evidence from PIAAC Data", *OECD Economics Department Working Papers*, No. 1209, OECD Publishing, Paris, http://dx.doi.org/10.1787/5js1pzx1r2kb-en.

Adalet McGowan, M. and D. Andrews (2015b), "Skill Mismatch and Public Policy in OECD Countries", *OECD Economics Department Working Papers*, No. 1210, OECD Publishing, Paris, http://dx.doi.org/10.1787/5js1pzw9lnwk-en.

BIS – Business Innovation and Skills (2012), "Industrial Strategy: UK Sector Analysis (No. 18)", Department for Business Innovation and Skills.

Department of Basic Education (2013), *Macro Indicator Report*.

European Commission (2016), *European Innovation Scoreboard 2016*, European Union, Brussels.

Fauvelle-Aymar, C. (2014), "Migration and Employment in South Africa: An Econometric Analysis of Domestic and International Migrants (QLFS (Q3) 2012)", MiWORC Report, No. 6.

Green, F. (2016), "Skills Demand, Training and Skills Mismatch: A Review of Key Concepts, Theory and Evidence", UK Foresight Future of Skills and Lifelong Learning Project.

Home Office (2015), "Determining Labour Shortages and the Need for Labour Migration from Third Countries in the UK: European Migration Network Focused Study", Home Office Science.

Mullis, I.V.S. et al. (2012), "TIMSS 2011 International Results in Mathematics", TIMSS & PIRLS International Study Center, Chestnut Hill.

Observatorio de las Ocupaciones (2015), "2015 Informe del Mercado de Trabajo de los Extranjeros Estatal (Datos 2014)", Servicio Público de Empleo Estatal, Madrid.

OECD (2017a), *OECD Employment Outlook 2017*, OECD Publishing, Paris, http://dx.doi.org/10.1787/empl_outlook-2017-en.

OECD (2017b, forthcoming), *Getting Skills Right: South Africa*, OECD Publishing, Paris.

OECD (2017c, forthcoming), *Getting Skills Right: France*, OECD Publishing, Paris.

OECD (2017d, forthcoming), *Getting Skills Right: Italy*, OECD Publishing, Paris.

OECD (2017e, forthcoming), *Getting Skills Right: Spain*, OECD Publishing, Paris.

OECD (2017f, forthcoming), *Getting Skills Right: United Kingdom*, OECD Publishing, Paris.

OECD (2016a), *OECD Science, Technology and Industry Outlook 2014*, OECD Publishing, Paris, http://dx.doi.org/10.1787/sti_outlook-2014-en.

OECD (2016b), *OECD Employment Outlook 2016*, OECD Publishing, Paris, http://dx.doi.org/10.1787/empl_outlook-2016-en.

OECD (2016c), *Education at a Glance 2016: OECD Indicators*, OECD Publishing, Paris, http://dx.doi.org/10.187/eag-2016-en.

OECD (2016d), *Building Skills for All: A Review of England*, OECD Skills Studies, OECD, Paris, https://www.oecd.org/unitedkingdom/building-skills-for-all-review-of-england.pdf.

OECD (2015), *International Migration Outlook 2015*, OECD Publishing, Paris, http://dx.doi.org/10.1787/migr_outlook-2015-en.

OECD (2014), *OECD Employment Outlook 2014*, OECD Publishing, Paris, http://dx.doi.org/10.1787/empl_outlook-2014-en.

OECD (2012), *OECD Employment Outlook 2012*, OECD Publishing, Paris, http://dx.doi.org/10.1787/empl_outlook-2012-en.

Reddy, V. et al. (2012), *Highlights from TIMSS 2011: The South African perspective*, HSRC, Pretoria.

Rienzo, C. (2016), "Characteristics and Outcomes of Migrants in the UK Labour Market", The Migration Observatory, University of Oxford.

Salvatori, A. (2015), "The Anatomy of Job Polarisation in the UK", *IZA Discussion Paper*, No. 9193, IZA, Bonn. Statistics South Africa (2016), *Labour Market Dynamics in South Africa, 2015*, Statistics South Africa, Pretoria.

Statistics South Africa (2015), *Labour Market Dynamics in South Africa, 2014*, Statistics South Africa, Pretoria.

Wadsworth, J. (2015), "Immigration and the UK Labour Market", Centre for Economic Performance, London School of Economics and Political Science.

Chapter 2

Evidence from the *Skills for Jobs Database* and the state of skill imbalances today

Market forces should help align skills demand and skills supply. However, due to time inconsistencies, rigidities or information gaps, the response of skills supply to changing demand (and vice versa) can be slow, generating skill imbalances. Understanding where these skill imbalances arise is crucial to design effective policy responses. To assist policy makers in doing so, the OECD has developed the Skills for Jobs Database, providing objective and comparable measures of skill shortages and mismatch for all European countries and South Africa. This chapter provides a summary of key findings for the five countries reviewed.

Skills in shortage

The results emerging from the *OECD Skills for Jobs Database* (OECD, 2017) are in line with the general evidence of increasing importance of social and creative intelligence skills. The term, "social and creative intelligence skills" was coined by Frey and Osborne (2013) to identify tasks that cannot be carried out by robots or computers. Creative work involves the development of novel ideas and requires the ability to achieve desired goals without explicit instruction. Social intelligence involves a wealth of tacit knowledge about social and cultural contexts, including the ability to pick up on subtleties in behaviour that are difficult to specify and can give rise to misinterpretation.

Social and creative intelligence and STEM skills are in shortage in almost all countries reviewed. Figure 2.1 highlights how shortages are apparent in all five countries in skills related to either creativity (deductive and inductive reasoning and fluency of ideas) or social intelligence (co-operation and social perceptiveness). Other soft skills emerging as in shortage include adaptability, co-operation, initiative, leadership and persistency. Relatively large shortages in these skills emerge in Spain but also in the United Kingdom. This is less so in South Africa and Italy where the demand for low-level skills is still rife. While the demand for high-level skills is still limited in Spain based on the indicators presented in Chapter 1, the supply is also very limited, generating the shortages shown in Figure 2.1.

Shortages are also apparent in STEM-related skills, particularly in Spain and France. The exception is South Africa where, as shown above, limited innovation potential is likely to limit demand for these skills.

Figure 2.1. Skill shortages in social and creative intelligence skills exist in all countries

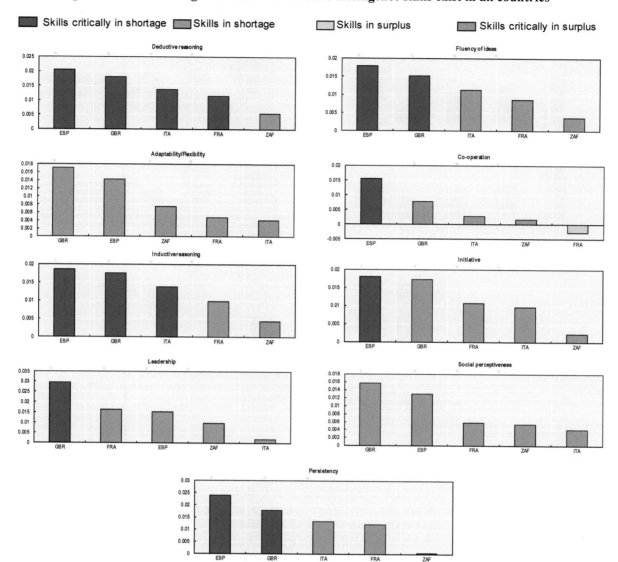

Note: Latest available year. Critical shortage (dark blue) is defined as the observations in the top quartile of positive skill imbalance values across countries and skills. Critical surplus (dark grey) is defined as the observations in the bottom quartile of the negative values. Values for the Ability dimension range from -0.025 and 0.035 across countries.

Source: OECD Skills for Jobs Database (2017).

Figure 2.2. Strong demand for STEM-related skills is also evidence in most countries except South Africa

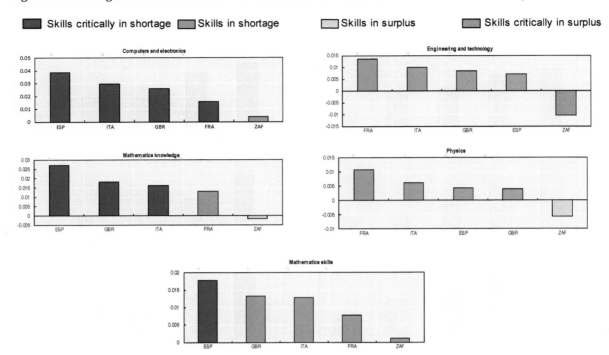

Note: Latest available year. Critical shortage (dark blue) is defined as the observations in the top quartile of positive skill imbalance values across countries and skills. Critical surplus (dark grey) is defined as the observations in the bottom quartile of the negative values. Values for the Knowledge dimension range from -0.040 and 0.056 across countries.

Source: OECD Skills for Jobs Database (2017).

Skills in surplus

Surpluses of low-level skills are frequent, particularly in Spain, South Africa and the United Kingdom. The *Skills for Jobs Database* also shows that skill surpluses tend to emerge in routine physical skills. This is in line with the reduced demand for these skills in the context of digitalisation and globalisation trends, but also with excess supply in some countries, notably Spain and South Africa. Interestingly, for the countries reviewed, the database indicates some surpluses in dexterity skills, while Frey and Osborne (2013) classify perception and manipulation as skills for which demand should remain rife as they cannot easily be reproduced by technology. This discrepancy might be the result of subtle differences in the way these skills are defined. In our database, dexterity is defined as fine motor skills, e.g. the ability to quickly move the hand to manipulate an object, or to make precisely co-ordinated movements of the fingers. On the other hand, Frey and Osborne's definition of perception and manipulation tasks implies a higher degree of complexity. They define perception and manipulation tasks as those requiring the depth and breadth of human perception, which are made more complex by unstructured work environments and the requirement to handle irregular objects.

Figure 2.3. Surpluses concentrate on low-level skills

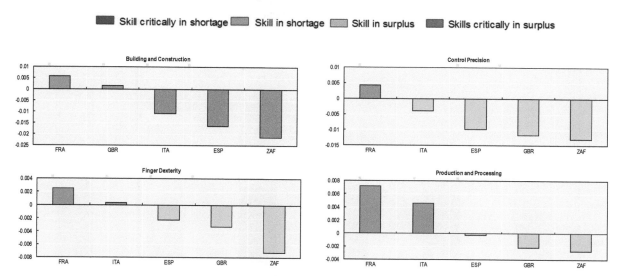

Note: Latest available year. Critical shortage (dark blue) is defined as the observations in the top quartile of positive skill imbalance values across countries and skills. Critical surplus (dark grey) is defined as the observations in the bottom quartile of the negative values. Values for the ability dimensions (e.g. finger dexterity and control precision) range from -0.025 and 0.035 across countries. Values for the knowledge dimension (e.g. building and construction, and production and processing) range from -0.040 to 0.056 across countries.

Source: OECD Skills for Jobs Database (2017).

Skill mismatches

Mismatches are pervasive, affecting between a third and a half of workers. Mismatch can be measured both vertically and horizontally. Vertical mismatch measures the degree to which individuals work in jobs for which they are over-qualified or underqualified, while horizontal mismatch assesses whether a person is working in the same field as the one they specialised in during school. Horizontal and vertical mismatch at work are common in all five countries. Vertical mismatch is particularly high in South Africa where it affects over half of workers, with about 30% of workers possessing qualifications higher than those required by their job and another 25% lacking an adequate certificate. The least affected country, based on the *Skills for Jobs Database*, is France with 23% of overqualified workers and 12% of underqualified workers. Horizontal mismatch – the discrepancy between a workers' field of study and the type of work he does – varies less across countries, ranging between 33% in South Africa and 40% in the United Kingdom.

Figure 2.4. Horizontal and vertical qualification imbalances are widespread

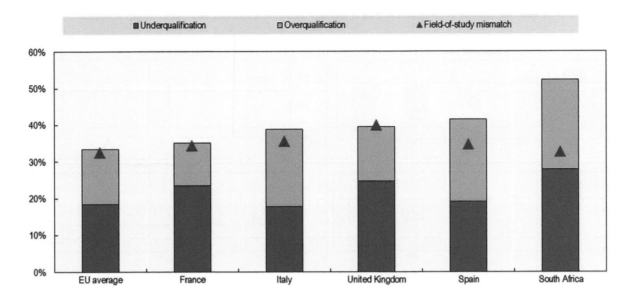

Source: *OECD Skills for Jobs Database* (2017).

Implications for skills imbalances

As mentioned above and as stressed in OECD (2017g), *persistent skills mismatches and shortages entail large costs for individuals, employers and society.* They can result in lower earnings and job satisfaction, higher risk of job loss, loss of competitiveness as well as lower economic growth.

At the individual level, skill mismatch has a negative impact on job satisfaction and wages (Montt, 2015; OECD, 2013). At the firm level, skill mismatch has been associated with lower productivity, and increased on-the-job search and turnover, while skill shortages have been shown to increase the cost of hiring and hinder the adoption of new technologies (OECD, 2012). At the macroeconomic level, mismatch increases structural unemployment, reduces economic output relative to potential output (Sattinger, 1993), and reduces GDP growth via misallocation of human capital (Adalet McGowan and Andrews, 2015), while skill shortages have equally adverse effects on labour productivity (OECD, 2012). In light of these costs, the remainder of the report highlights policy challenges and solutions to effectively tackle and reduce existing skills imbalances.

References

Adalet McGowan, M. and D. Andrews (2015), "Labour Market Mismatch and Labour Productivity: Evidence from PIAAC Data", *OECD Economics Department Working Papers*, No. 1209, OECD Publishing, Paris, http://dx.doi.org/10.1787/5js1pzx1r2kb-en.

Frey, C. and M. Osborne (2013), "The Future of Employment: How Susceptible are Jobs to Computerisation?", Oxford Martin School.

Montt, G. (2015), "The Causes and Consequences of Field-of-study Mismatch: An Analysis Using PIAAC", *OECD Social, Employment and Migration Working Papers*, No. 167, OECD Publishing, Paris, http://dx.doi.org/10.1787/5jrxm4dhv9r2-en.

OECD (2017), *Getting Skills Right: Skills for Jobs Indicators*, OECD Publishing, Paris.

OECD (2013), *Skills Outlook: First Results from the Survey of Adult Skills*, Paris: OECD Publishing

OECD (2012), *OECD Employment Outlook 2012*, OECD Publishing, Paris, http://dx.doi.org/10.1787/empl_outlook-2012-en.

Sattinger, M. (1993), "Assignment Models of the Distribution of Earnings", *Journal of Economic Literature*, Vol. 31, pp. 831-880.

Chapter 3

How countries assess skill imbalances

To be successful, policy intervention to address skill mismatch and skill shortages requires access to high-quality information about the current and future skill needs of the labour market. The OECD Skills for Jobs Database *can assist policy makers in responding to skill imbalances, and this information should be integrated with other skill assessment and anticipation exercises (SAA) carried out in each country to respond to specific information needs, notably at the sectoral and geographical levels. The reviewed countries vary by the nature of these exercises, the involvement of stakeholders and the use of the outcomes in policy making. This chapter identifies key differences in the type of exercises conducted and stakeholders' involvement in the five countries reviewed, and puts forward examples of good practice to improve the production and use of skill needs information.*

Who assesses skill needs

In all five countries concerned, the government plays a key role in collecting information on skill needs. However, in many cases, special bodies are tasked to carry out the assessment. In France, France Stratégie – a government think-tank overseen by the Prime Minister's office – carries out employment forecasting exercises in conjunction with the research branch of the Ministry of Labour (DARES). These exercises generate, for each occupation, the number of projected job openings, and hence allow identifying occupations in strong demand. Similarly, ISFOL (now INAPP) played until recently a key role in the collection of skill needs information in Italy. Placed under the responsibility of the Ministry of Labour, ISFOL regularly carried out an employer survey – the Audit of Occupational Needs – the results of which are disseminated through a web portal on Professions, Employment and Skill Requirements. The responsibilities of ISFOL, which has recently been dismantled, have been passed on to its successor INAPP. A slightly different model is followed in the United Kingdom where the production and co-ordination of skill needs assessment exercises used to be the responsibility of the UK Commission for Employment and Skills (UKCES): a publicly-funded, industry-led organisation that provided guidance on skills and employment issues. UKCES produced two major employer-based surveys: the Employer Skills Survey (ESS) and the Employer Perspectives Survey (EPS). The UKCES also oversaw a "Working Futures" model that generated long-term macro-economic projections of employment demand by sector, occupation and qualification level. The commission was dismantled in March 2017 and some of the exercises it used to carry out are now under the responsibility of the Department of Education.

The situation is different in South Africa, where the main assessment exercise is carried out by the Department for Higher Education and Training (DHET). The DHET produces an annual list of top 100 occupations in high demand, using a combination of data analysis, econometric modelling, literature reviews and stakeholder engagement.

In Spain, the public employment service, *Servicio Público de Empleo Estatal* (SEPE), produces a catalogue of hard-to-fill occupations on a quarterly basis (*el catálogo de ocupaciones de difícil cobertura*). The list is prepared using data collected from the regional public employment services for each province and region. The public employment service also plays a central role in France where it collects information on job searchers and job openings and also runs a survey of existing and foreseen hiring needs (*Besoins en Main-d'œuvre*).

Finally, sectoral and regional skill needs are assessed: in France through the *Centre Animation Ressources d'Information sur la Formation / Observatoire Régional Emploi Formation* and the *Observatoires Prospectives des Métiers et Qualifications* (OPMQs); in the United Kingdom through Sector Skills Councils; and in South Africa through the Sector Employment and Training Authorities.

The type of skills assessment and anticipation exercises

Exercises range from econometric models to composite indices to recruitment difficulties surveys. The nature of exercises varies widely, with several types conducted in each of the countries examined. For instance, many initiatives rely on a mix of information from econometric exercises, job vacancies information, wage and employment pressures and foresight exercises. This is the case, notably, for the assessments carried out by France Stratégie in France, by DHET in South Africa, and by the Migration Advisory Committee in the United Kingdom.

Assessments based on a single method also exist: the Working Futures model in the United Kingdom and the estimates generated by the Italian Chamber of Commerce

(UNIONCAMERE) rely primarily on econometric modelling. Other exercises rely primarily on employer surveys of recruitment difficulties, including the *Observatoire Tendance Emploi Compétence* (Observatoire TEC) run by an association of employer organisations in France, an assessment conducted by UNIONCAMERE in Italy, and the Annual Labour Survey run by the Ministry of Employment and Social Security in Spain.

Studies which trace the employment outcomes of graduates over time are carried out in France, Italy, Spain, and pilot studies have been introduced in South Africa and the United Kingdom. These graduate tracer studies are a good source of information of labour market demand for specific occupations and to provide career guidance to prospective students. In Italy, Almalaurea carries out an annual national survey on the employability of university graduates; in France, the Cerèq follows school leavers over time through the *Enquête génération*, a cohort study of young people leaving initial education. In Spain, the Ministry of Education, Culture and Sports (MECD) conducts the "Labour Market Entrance of University graduates: the Social Security membership perspective*" (Inserción laboral de los egresados universitarios: La perspectiva de la afiliación a la Seguridad Social*), which uses social security affiliation data to track employment and earnings outcomes of a cohort of university students who graduate in 2010 for four years after they graduate. Another graduate study is conducted in Spain by the National Institute of Statistics. This Labour Market Entrance of University Graduates Survey (*Encuesta de Inserción laboral de titulados universitarios*) combines administrative data and interviews with university graduates. Tracer studies have also been implemented in South Africa, though these have been limited in scope. The Labour Market Intelligence Partnership (LMIP) has been experimenting with new tracer studies across different sectors (university, TVET college, community college and workplace learning), making substantial progress in standardising research methodologies and identifying how these studies could be institutionalised (Rogan, 2016).

Mechanisms used for stakeholder involvement and co-ordination

As skills imbalances affect a number of different actors, it is critical to involve a representative group of stakeholders in their assessment, anticipation and policy response. However, the level of stakeholder involvement varies significantly across countries and so do the mechanisms put in place to enhance collaboration and co-ordination among the relevant parties.

In the United Kingdom, the UKCES used to play a key co-ordination role in the production of skills intelligence. France envisages a similar role for the *Réseau Emploi Compétences* (REC), to bring together different providers of skills needs exercises and decision makers from related fields. The objective of the REC is precisely to create a dialogue between the different players at the national, regional and sectoral level, to strengthen the diffusion of knowledge between the players, and to reinforce co-operation through joint projects.

The Italian Institute of Statistics (ISTAT) and ISFOL have recently put major efforts into developing an inter-institutional partnership with the intent of improving synergies across different data sources that, directly or indirectly, can provide key information about skill needs in Italy. This *Sistema Informativo sulle Professioni* (Information System on Occupations) aims to aggregate labour market intelligence from several institutions. The idea is to provide final users (e.g. policy makers, end-users, officials in the various ministries) precious labour market information at the occupational level.

Examples of good practice in the co-ordination of skill needs assessments outside the reviewed countries are provided in Box 3.1.

Box 3.1. Examples of good practice in the co-ordination of skill needs assessment

In most countries, a series of ministries, government agencies, regional and sub-regional administrative levels and social partners are involved in the discussions of results from skills assessment and anticipation exercises. They are also involved in the development of an appropriate policy response. The number of actors as well as the diversity of interests and institutional objectives may make it difficult to reach consensus when deciding, first, what the skills needs are and, second, on the most appropriate policy response to these needs. Enabling dialogue between stakeholders is an obvious first step. It may be hindered, however, by the limited time availability from agencies and stakeholders to take part in conversations, by the changing priorities and resources of different agencies and by the need for agencies to find mutual benefit to collaboration and avoiding duplication of work. Even when collaboration takes place, agreement on skills needs and policy responses may still be difficult.

Several mechanisms exist across countries to facilitate consensus-building and overcome potential conflict among stakeholders involved in the assessment of skill needs. These include involving stakeholders in the advisory boards of key agencies or actively involving them through thematic workshops. Other consensus-reaching mechanisms include developing a legal framework that articulates the engagement of different stakeholders in the process; involving high-level political representatives; and articulating the discussions around very concrete and short-term objectives.

Special bodies to foster collaboration among stakeholders exist in a number of countries. Advisory boards involving ministries and social partners exist in Denmark and Wallonia (Belgium). Participation of stakeholders in the agency carrying out the skills assessment exercises can ensure a common understanding of future skills needs and the long-term economic environment (e.g. Norway, Finland). In Ireland, independent bodies, the Expert Group on Future Skills Needs (EGFSN) and the Further Education and Training Authority (SOLAS), are in charge of skills assessment and anticipation exercises and involve ministries, regional agencies and other public bodies. EGFSN also involves social partners and reports to the ministries of Employment and Education. Inter-ministerial collaboration (and collaboration with stakeholders) in employment and vocational training policies has improved in recent years in Portugal, largely due to the efforts of ANQEP, an agency established under the supervision of the Ministry of Education and Science and the Ministry of Solidarity Employment and Social Security, in co-operation with the Ministry of Economy (OECD, 2015). The success of stakeholder participation in these special bodies is facilitated in countries where a long tradition of social dialogue exists. Where this is not the case, a National Skills Strategy can act as a framework for consensus-building and for guiding the discussions around a common objective of improving skills development and use in the country.

Workshops and conferences also provide opportunities for stakeholders' discussions. In Canada, and in response to the perplexities expressed by employers in response to official forecasts, the Department of Employment and Social Development (ESDC) has engaged with stakeholders directly or in ad-hoc workshops to provide a better understanding of the forecasts and what they can and cannot do. In Norway, narrowly-themed conferences promote consensus reaching, as was the case of a conference on skills needs in the engineering sector and another one on skills brought by immigrant workers.

In some countries, formal mandates are issued in specific legislative acts to foster dialogue among stakeholders. In the United States, the Workforce Innovation and Opportunity Act (WIOA), signed in 2014, consolidates job training programmes into a single funding stream. Among other provisions, it promotes greater and better consultation among federal agencies, in particular the Department of Labor and the Department of Education, and requires collaboration between agencies at the state level through joint strategic planning efforts. In the Netherlands, the mandate of the agency in charge of implementing employment insurance (UWV) and providing labour and data services calls for it to ensure transparency in the labour market, and that no barriers hinder the collaboration and co-ordination with stakeholders. The new skills assessment and anticipation exercise in the Czech Republic (PŘEKVAP) will include provisions for the organisation of dialogue between stakeholders.

Finally, ensuring high-level political engagement and setting specific objectives and policy priorities has helped inter-ministerial collaboration in the United States, Estonia and the Netherlands.

Source: OECD (2017), *Getting Skills Right: Assessing and Anticipating Changing Skills Needs.*

The use of skill needs information in policy making

A crucial challenge for many OECD countries is that of making the best use of skills assessment and anticipation information. OECD (2017) provides a comprehensive analysis of the different skill assessment and anticipation systems across a wide variety of countries. That analysis, moreover, provides examples of how the information collected is used for policy making in various areas such as employment, education or even migration policy.

OECD (2017) shows that governments in OECD countries use the information to update occupational standards; to design or revise training policies for workers or the unemployed; to design, revise or decide on the allocation of courses to provide in formal education, with this information being used in many countries to inform the development of vocational education and training programmes or apprenticeships. In addition, some governments use this information to guide migration policy as well as their transition to a digital or green economy. Social partners also use this information to lobby governments on education and employment policy, develop training programmes, or provide advice to their members on skill development. Both social partners and governments use this information for broad dissemination purposes to inform workers and students about trends in current or future skill demand and supply.

In France, Spain, South Africa and the United Kingdom, skill needs information feeds into migration policies. In the United Kingdom the data is used by the Migration Advisory Committee, a non-governmental public body commissioned by the UK Government to develop and periodically review the high-skill shortage occupation list that governs Tier 2 (i.e. skilled workers with a job offer) immigration decisions for non-EU work migrants. Similarly, Spain facilitates entry of foreigners who are in occupations listed on the catalogue of hard-to-fill occupations, although, since the 2008 crisis, hardly any occupations have made it onto this list. In South Africa, the list of occupations in high demand compiled by DHET is used by the Department of Home Affairs to develop its list of critical skills for issuing the Critical Skills Visa. Finally, in France, the Dares' skills pressure indicator is used to determine the list of occupations for which labour migration is more flexible.

Quality information on skill needs should be crucial in the planning of training provision. Surprisingly, at the government level, this is only the case in France where the public employment service (*Pôle Emploi*) estimates training needs based on information on expected recruitments from the BMO survey. These estimated training needs are used to decide on the amount and type of training to procure for the unemployed. However, sectoral bodies and unions do collect and/or use skill needs information to plan training provision in other countries. For instance, Sector Skills Councils in the United Kingdom used to be instrumental in organising apprenticeships and facilitating linkages between training providers and firms, presumably based on the information on skill needs they help to collect. To a large extent, this role has now been taken up by employer-led trailblazer panels (see Chapter 4 in this report) In Spain, trade unions use skill needs information to develop / fund up-skilling or re-skilling programmes for union members and to develop / fund apprenticeship or work-experience programmes.

In some countries, skill needs information informs career guidance. This is the case in France where the skills pressure information is used by several regions to provide career guidance. Also, in South Africa, the DHET uses the list to provide career guidance, through specialised leaflets and their career advice portal (NCAP). In Spain, the public employment service circulates the list of occupations in high demand on a regular basis to career guidance counsellors by email.

In Italy, use of skill needs data in policy making has been somewhat limited in the past but the recent education, employment and industrial reforms seem to be firmly based in the use of the rich available SAA information. Furthermore, the involvement of the ministry of employment in the activities of the ISFOL/INAPP promises more continuity in analysis of skill needs. At the same time, the engagement of the ministry of education and research (MIUR) and the ministry of economic development (MISE) in creating a solid information network (*Sistema Informativo sulle Professioni*) with ISTAT represents a case of best practice that should be strengthened even further through the engagement of other relevant ministries.

Incentives and support for skills assessment exercises

In some of the countries, only a limited number of employers analyse and evaluate their skills needs on a regular basis. When employers understand their existing and future skills needs, they can better anticipate and plan their training and hiring decisions. While firms are often encouraged to undertake skills need exercises through skill levy systems, further incentives might be needed, especially for smaller firms.

France introduced a number of mechanisms to encourage the collection of better skill needs information from employers. Big firms (employing at least 300 employees) are required to do an analysis of their skill needs at least once every three years, and negotiate on the required actions with the social partners (*Gestion Prévisionnelle des Emplois et Compétences*, GPEC). The analysis generally involves a stock-taking exercise of available skills, and a forecast of future skills needs based on medium- and long-term strategies. Based on this analysis, the firm can decide on possible tools to overcome anticipated shortages, such as training investment and professional mobility, after consultation with the social partners. This requirement does not hold for smaller firms, but government-funded financial aid is available for small firms wanting to do a skills need exercise. An enterprise survey focussed on SMEs showed that 16% of the surveyed firms use the GPEC and 36% use similar tools to assess their skill needs (Ministère de l'Economie, des Finances et de l'Industrie, 2005).

To help sectors and regions in identifying skill needs, the French Government introduced a contract for prospective exercises (*Contrat d'Etudes Prospectives*). This contract is signed between the government and professional organisations, and can be co-signed by labour organisations and regional organisations. In many cases, social partners are involved through the Occupations and Qualifications Observatories which they are encouraged to set up. The main goals of the contract are i) to develop a better understanding of employment, occupations and qualifications, and their evolution, ii) to develop medium-term forecasts, and iii) to propose actions to address the current and upcoming changes. Under this contract the government provides a subsidy to help finance the analysis, which should be done by an external party. When the scale of the project is too small to be eligible for a contract for prospective exercise, it is possible to get technical support (*appui technique*) for sectoral or regional diagnoses of skills needs.

A very different model was used in the United Kingdom, where *the UK Commission for Employment and Skills used to produce and co-ordinate skill needs assessment exercises.* Notably, the commission outlined a common framework approach for all Sector Skill Councils to follow when collecting this data, which facilitated comparison of labour market performance between sectors. To carry out skill needs data collection, Sector Skill Councils were originally funded by the government through a system of grants. However, the funding system was changed in 2012 in an effort to foster greater employer leadership and co-investment. Sector Skill Councils now charge membership fees to firms that can afford to contribute, although the councils provide services to all firms within a given sector.

References

Ministère de l'Economie, des Finances et de l'Industrie (2005), *Le développement du capital humain dans les entreprises*, France.

OECD (2017), *Getting Skills Right: Assessing and Anticipating Changing Skill Needs*, OECD Publishing, Paris, http://dx.doi.org/10.1787/9789264252073-en.

OECD (2015), "OECD Skills Strategy Diagnostic Report: Portugal", OECD, Paris, https://www.oecd.org/skills/nationalskillsstrategies/Portugal-Executive-Summary-web.pdf.

Rogan, M. (2016), "Tracing Graduates into the Labour Market", *HSRC Review*, Vol. 15, No. 3.

Chapter 4

Policies to reduce skill imbalances

Skills imbalances have become a widespread concern among policy makers. Beyond the assessment and anticipation of skill needs in an attempt to prevent skill imbalances, governments are focusing on finding solutions for those imbalances that inevitably arise. Actions to foster a better matching between supply and demand span education, lifelong learning, and active and passive labour market policies. Action may be needed on several fronts, including policies which target the demand for skills, their supply, or both. In some of the countries reviewed, shortages in high-level skills are motivated by high unmet demand, while in others they arise because of limited supply.

This chapter provides examples and insights into the practical ways in which governments can improve matching of the skills and qualifications that are available in the labour market, with those that employers need. In the next chapter, a set of best practice principles are provided to guide the design of policies to reduce skill imbalances.

Education and training: Policies targeting employers

Employers have much to gain from investing in the skills of their workforce, including higher productivity and lower turnover. But due to a number of market failures, actual employer investment in training may be sub-optimal and government intervention could be warranted. Policies are in place in many countries to encourage employers to get involved in vocational education: by contributing input into curriculum development, financing the classroom portion of apprenticeship training, and offering work placements for the work-based component of apprenticeship training. Training levies can also encourage employers to invest in adult learning that meets their skill needs, more generally.

Vocational education

Employer involvement in the development of vocational education curriculum is critical. The ability of vocational education and work-based learning programmes to deliver skills required in the labour market depends on inputs from employers. Employer engagement in vocational education is critical to ensure that the curriculum reflects the needs of the labour market and that enough work placements are available, in the case of work-based learning programmes. In England, under the new apprenticeship standards, employer-led panels called "trailblazers" will now decide the requirements of apprenticeships and set their assessment plans. This reform follows in the tradition of world-class apprenticeship systems like those in Switzerland, where educational institutions work closely with industry associations to develop apprenticeship curriculum frameworks.

Some countries impose levies on employers to finance the classroom portion of apprenticeship training. As employers stand to benefit the most from the availability of a pool of candidates with relevant skills, levies are seen as a fair way to have them share in the cost. In 2017, England instituted an "apprenticeship levy" to incentivise employer investment in apprenticeship training. All employers with a pay bill of at least GBP 3 million are required to pay a levy equal to 0.5% of their annual pay bill in excess of GBP 3 million. These funds go into a digital account that can be spent by employers on the class-based component of apprenticeship training for new and existing employees. In France, too, employers contribute to the financing of the class-based component of apprenticeships through an apprenticeship tax which amounts to 0.68% of the firm's wage bill. Employers decide which training centres or schools receive their tax funding. By participating in the cost of the class-based component of apprenticeship training, employers may also assume higher responsibility for the curriculum content.

Countries also offer financial incentives to promote the apprenticeship contract among employers. To encourage employers to participate in apprenticeships, some countries offer subsidies or tax incentives. For example, in Spain, employers can deduct training costs from their social security contributions when they sign training and apprenticeship contracts (*los contratos para formación y aprentizaje*) which commit employers to provide the trainee (age 16-30) with a job related to their vocational training qualification for up to three years. A similar type of relief from paying social security contributions for apprentices is available to employers in the United Kingdom and France. It is also common for employers to receive additional subsidies for hiring young apprentices. For instance, UK employers receive a grant when they hire apprentices between the ages of 16 and 24, while French employers can count on subsidies if they hire apprentices aged 18 or younger. Beyond subsidies for hiring young apprentices, France also offers employers tax credits for hiring apprentices who are low-skilled, and apprenticeship hiring subsidies which specifically target small firms.

Beyond financial incentives, small and medium-sized enterprises (SME) may require technical support to be able to offer an apprenticeship programme. SMEs face greater barriers to hiring apprentices than larger firms, including difficulty articulating their training needs, lack of training infrastructure, inadequate teaching expertise, and ignorance about classroom training programmes. As a result, their participation in apprenticeships is lower. Providing support to SMEs in developing apprenticeship programmes can help to raise their participation. In Spain, for example, two NGOs (Fundación Bertelsmann and the JP Morgan Chase Foundation) collaborated to provide free technical support to SMEs interested in developing an apprenticeship programme. The pilot initiative focused on firms with between 10 and 500 employees. A consulting team worked with 190 SMEs to advise them through the process of creating apprenticeship places, including identifying positions within the company which could be filled by apprentices and matching available VET qualifications with firm's skill needs. Of the 190 firms that the team worked with, 115 expect to offer at least one apprenticeship position during 2016/17 and 2017/18 – suggesting that technical support can help SMEs to overcome non-financial barriers in providing apprenticeships.

Training levies

South Africa's training levy steers employers to invest in high-demand skills, though administrative burden affects take-up. In South Africa, France, and Spain, employers are required to pay a levy to fund training opportunities for their employees. In South Africa, a skills development levy of 1% of the total annual wage bill must be paid by all firms with an annual wage bill of at least ZAR 500 000. Firms must submit workplace skills plans (WSP) and annual training reports (ATR) which outline their skill requirements and how their provision of training succeeded in addressing them, in order to recoup their levy funds. About 40% of levy funds are earmarked for so-called PIVOTAL grants, which refer to professional, vocational, technical and academic programmes that address scarce and critical skill needs. Training funded by PIVOTAL grants must be provided at accredited institutions. However, few firms recoup their skill levy funds since they fail to submit their WSPs and ATRs. Low take-up may be due to the cumbersome process involved in completing these reports, which can be time-consuming.

On the other hand, Spain's levy places few burdens on employers, but at the cost of more spending on mandatory workplace training rather than addressing skill needs. In Spain, the professional training levy (*Cotización para formación professional*) is a contribution of 0.7% of a company's payroll, of which 0.6% is borne by employers and 0.1% is borne by workers. About a third of the collected levy funds are available to employers to fund programmes for their own employees, while the remaining funds go to programmes to train the unemployed, public administration workers, and other workers. To use levy funds, employers receive credits which are valued at a percentage of their levy payment, and small employers can co-ordinate to aggregate training credits. Employers may use the credits to conduct training internally, to hire an external provider or to collaborate with other employers to submit joint bids for common training programmes. Individual employees can also apply to their employer for *Permisos Individuales de Formación*, which grants the worker paid time off to pursue accredited vocational training, while the employer is compensated for lost wages. Employers must submit training bids to the State Foundation for Professional Training (*Fundación Estatal para la Formación en el Empleo*) at least one week before the start of the course, and training must last a minimum of two hours. Other than verifying that training is legitimate and meets these minimum requirements, though, Fundación Estatal places no restrictions on the type of training that can be covered by levy funds. As a result, most firms use them to pay for mandatory workplace training, like health and hygiene, rather than addressing skill needs (Figure 4.1). This relative freedom to spend levy funds in Spain contrasts starkly with South Africa, where employers must demonstrate through WSPs and ATRs that training provision addresses their skill needs, and where a portion of levy funds are earmarked for generating scarce and critical skills (i.e. the PIVOTAL grants). Restricting spending of levy funds to scarce skills and to training provided by accredited institutions, as is done in South Africa, helps to ensure that employers invest in training which meets their skill needs. On the other hand, an overly burdensome process for recouping levy funds should be avoided, as this may lower take-up.

Figure 4.1. Few requirements on how levy funds can be spent mean that most training firms in Spain use levy funds for mandatory workplace training

Share of training firms, by type of training activity, 2015

Type of training	Share of training firms
Mandatory workplace training (health or hygiene)	60.2
Job-specific training	43.2
Other	24.4
Customer service	20.9
Team work	14.4
Office administration	13.3
Management	11.6
Foreign language training	11.4
Information technology - general	10.3
Problem-solving	8.3
Information technology - specialised	5.0
Basic literacy and numeracy	2.0

Share of employees trained, by type of training activity, 2015

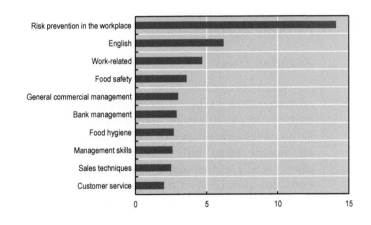

Source: Encuesta Anual Laboral, 2015. Formación en las Empresas.

Note: This chart shows the top ten training activities with the highest participation.

Source: Fundación Estatal para la Formación en el Empleo. Informe anual 2015. Formación en las empresas.

Education and training: Policies targeting individuals

Investment in education and training is needed to meet the increasing demand for skilled workers that most OECD countries have experienced. But in addition to *more* skills, investing in the *right* skills is equally important. Career guidance services and targeted financial incentives can encourage the development of high-demand skills. Facilitating lifelong learning among adults is also important, in order to promote resiliency in the face of technological change. Finally, incentives to invest in training are strengthened by well-developed systems of recognition of prior learning.

Career guidance services

Career guidance services can help steer individuals towards careers or training pathways for which they are well-suited and for which employment prospects are good, provided such services are informed by relevant and up-to-date labour market information. Each of the countries reviewed makes labour market information available online via a career guidance website. Several features of effective career guidance websites stand out. They include information on many different types of jobs, clarifying which qualifications are needed to perform the job, employment prospects, salary estimates and progression possibilities. Information is displayed as easy-to-read summary statistics, rather than long, dense reports. For example, Figure 4.2 shows a screenshot from Italy's *Eduscopio* website which makes use of visually attractive and colourful infographics to convey information simply and concisely. Longitudinal data of employment and salary outcomes of graduates are more informative for prospective students than average employment rates by qualification, as the latter conflates the impacts of age and experience. For example, Spain feeds their national careers guidance websites with longitudinal data of this type. Finally, good career guidance websites bolster information about particular occupations with links to current vacancies in that occupation, as is done in England's *National Career Service* and France's *PES Météo de l'Emploi* websites.

Figure 4.2. Italy's career guidance website showcases attractive infographics

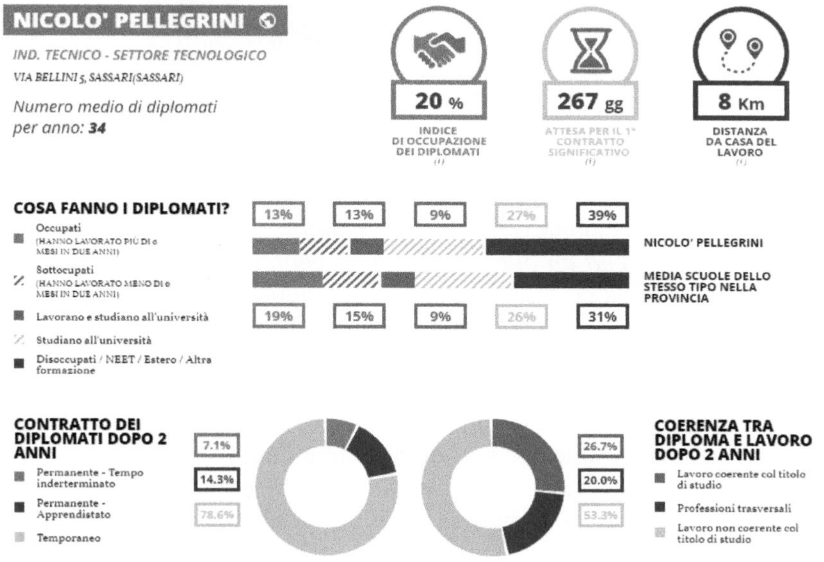

Source: Eduscopio website (https://eduscopio.it/).

Students do not receive sufficient information about education programmes and job opportunities in secondary school. Despite more information becoming available online, only 20% of young people in France think they are getting good career advice at their secondary school, compared with 23% in Spain and the United Kingdom, and 26% in Italy (see Figure 4.3). Even fewer feel like they receive sufficient information on job opportunities. A key challenge to providing better quality career guidance services to students is ensuring that career guidance specialists are informed about the full range of educational pathways available, and their labour market prospects. All countries reviewed struggle with a bias against vocational education relative to general academic programmes, which influences the career advice that career guidance specialists (not to mention, parents) provide. All countries in this review could benefit from offering regular workshops to career guidance specialists to brief them on which occupations are in demand, and which qualifications or fields of study would equip students to fill vacancies in those occupations. For example, the Swedish public employment service offers regular workshops to teachers which provide an overview of findings from their skill forecasts and assessment of skill needs. These presentations educate teachers about the types of occupations and skills most in demand, and make suggestions for how to diffuse labour market information to students.

Figure 4.3. Few young people think they are getting good career advice in secondary school

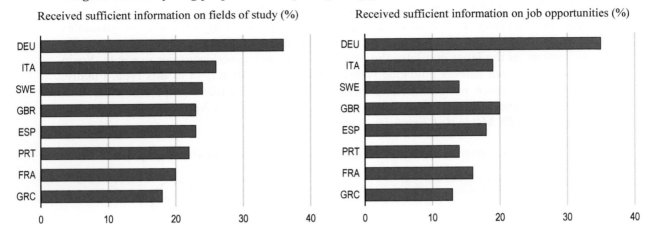

Source: McKinsey Survey, Aug-Sept 2012, 2013.

Repeated interactions with employers during secondary school are shown to reduce the likelihood that a student will end up outside of employment, education and training (NEET). Employer interactions like work visits, internships, employer-judged science fairs, and mentoring can be motivating experiences for students which clarify their career paths and strengthen their commitment to education and training. These types of activities are also beneficial to employers, as they provide an opportunity to shape their future skill pool and to build relationships with potential future hires. However, countries face challenges, first, in building employer involvement into the school curriculum and, second, in forging sufficient links with employers. France addresses the first challenge by building employer involvement directly into the curriculum in a formalised way. Throughout their years in secondary education, French students must have: i) participated in one organised firm visit; ii) met one professional from the world of work (e.g. attended a presentation given by employee or self-employed person about his or her job or sector); iii) participated in one supported project (e.g. setting up a student business); and iv) finished a compulsory internship. French students can track their activities related to the world of work using an application called "'Folios". With respect to the second challenge – that of forging links between employers and schools – England's Careers and Enterprise Company (CEC) sets a promising example. Established by the Department for Education, CEC receives funding from government to boost employer engagement in schools. The CEC is currently working with one half of secondary schools and colleges in England to develop "employer engagement plans," which chart plans to increase employer involvement in concrete ways, including employer visits, mentoring programmes, and employer advisory boards that give local business a say in the skills young people are taught.

Some countries offer career guidance services to adults to provide them with support when they consider changing careers. In France, for instance, the Advice for Professional Evolution (*Conseil en Évolution Professionnelle*, CEP) was launched in 2014, offering free and personalised career advice for people considering a career change. Adults can benefit from an individual meeting to analyse their professional situation, and obtain advice and support in defining and implementing their career change. The CEP is available for all employed and unemployed individuals, and employees can participate without having to inform their employer. Similarly, in Belgium, Flemish careers advice vouchers (*loopbaancheques)* entitle all employees and self-employed to eight hours of subsidised careers advice every six years. Vouchers for career guidance services must be purchased online, and 93% of costs are subsidised. During a personal assessment meeting with a counsellor, adults complete exercises and tasks to discover their strengths, job values, and career goals. Next, the individual and counsellor together establish a personal development plan, which outlines the steps needed to reach the career goal. Individuals who require additional support after the completion of eight hours of guidance (e.g. about how to implement their personal development plan) have access to one hour of free "post-guidance services". Employees have confidence that their privacy is assured and there will be no exchange between the career guidance centre and their employer. While these career guidance programmes could be costly to implement, they could pay off by assisting workers affected by redundancies into new types of work. Indeed, evidence suggests that the effects of financial incentives to invest in skills are likely to be strengthened when accompanied by guidance, counselling, or other support services (OECD, 2017).

Student bursaries

Some countries offer financial incentives to students to steer them towards high-demand skills and occupations in order to reduce skill mismatch and skill shortages. In England, universities receive endowments from public bodies to offer students bursaries for particular subjects, many of which are linked to occupations in shortage. For example, the National Health Service provides bursaries to students in dental, medical or health care courses which are in high demand. Government bursaries are also available to students pursuing high-demand science, technology, engineering and mathematics (STEM) programmes, and are paired with paid summer work in the government intelligence agency. Finally, bursaries are available to prospective math and physics teachers, contingent on their commitment to teach for at least three years after graduation – a policy directed at alleviating teacher shortages in these subjects. In South Africa, too, bursary programmes target qualifications that face high demand in the labour market. The *Funza Lushaka Bursary Programme* from the Department of Basic Education focuses on teaching qualifications in areas of national priority. Students receiving these bursaries are required to teach in public schools for the same number of years as they receive the bursary. A second type of bursary is provided by the National Skills Fund (NSF), and targets university students with a study focus in a scarce skill area.

Lifelong learning

Lifelong learning opportunities enable retraining and upskilling in the face of changing skill demand. Most OECD countries offer free basic skills training to adults in order to improve their employability. Beyond this, many countries offer incentives for employed workers to continue learning, including training leave, training accounts and loans. Training programmes for the unemployed have been shown to improve employment prospects over the medium-to-long term, and effects are particularly strong for the long-term unemployed (Card et al., 2015). Finally, some countries have established systems to recognise informal or non-formal learning, in order to boost the signalling power of skills and improve skill matching.

Portable training rights in France promote training for workers in non-standard working arrangements. In 2015 France introduced an individual training account (*Compte*

Personnel de Formation, CPF*)* which credits each full-time worker with 24 hours of training leave each year during the first five years of the programme, and with 12 hours per year during the subsequent three years – up to a maximum of 150 training hours in total. Training hours can be used to acquire recognised qualifications or basic skills, or to take courses selected by Regional Councils and social partners, which often reflect foreseeable economic needs. If the training takes place during working hours, then the employee needs to obtain permission from her employer, and if approved, the employer covers their wages over the training period. An innovative feature of the CPF is that training hours are preserved upon job loss and transferable between employers. In the context of rising employment in non-standard forms of work across OECD countries (e.g. part-time work, casual work and temporary contracts), portability of training rights can help to promote training among workers who generally have shorter job tenure and receive less training from employers (OECD, 2015). Training accounts are shown to be most successful in steering individuals to invest in high-demand skills when they are accompanied by guidance (OECD, 2017). Indeed, as discussed above, France also offers free career guidance services to all adults, which can help to steer adults to use their training accounts to train in skills and qualifications which are in demand.

Social partners in the United Kingdom actively recruit low-skilled workers for training which helps to address inequality in lifelong learning. In most OECD countries, low-skilled adults are less likely to participate in training activities. Poor participation among low-skilled workers could be driven by a number of factors: inability to afford training costs, barriers to taking time off work, lack of access to employer-sponsored training, disillusionment with formal education, or ignorance about which skills are worth investing in. Training which directly targets low-skilled workers may therefore be needed. For example, in the United Kingdom, the *Union Learning Fund* offers training programmes which mainly target low-skilled workers. The Union Learning Fund is organised by trade unions, which subsidise learning activities that they identify as important for their members, in consultation with employers, employees and learning providers. Union learning representatives engage directly with low-skilled workers to recruit their participation. As a result of this active recruitment of low-skilled workers, participants are disproportionately older workers and those with no formal prior qualifications. Low-skilled learners achieve the most significant outcomes, with over two-thirds of learners with no previous qualification moving to a higher qualification level (Stuart et al., 2016).

Recognition of prior learning

Validation of non-formal and informal learning improves skill matching in the labour market by strengthening the signalling power of skills, making it easier for employers to identify which skills jobseekers already have. Higher value in the labour market also improves incentives for individuals to invest in learning by allowing them to capitalise on their investment. Recognition of prior learning (RPL) is particularly important in countries with high levels of underqualification (including France, South Africa and England), since many workers who are underqualified possess the skills required by their jobs because they have acquired them through experience or uncertified training, but are lacking a qualification to prove this. Not an issue as long as a worker remains with a given employer, underqualification may make job moves more difficult and lengthen unemployment or job search spells as prospective employers cannot observe uncertified skills. Both France and South Africa have systems to recognise learning acquired informally or non-formally but RPL does not exist or is not well-developed in England, Spain or Italy.

RPL systems in France and South Africa are well-developed. In France, social partners developed the CléA certificate in 2016 in order to assess and validate an individual's skills in seven domains: expression, calculation, computer use, ability to follow direction and teamwork, working independently and taking initiative, willingness to learn, and mastering basic rules (safety, environment, hygiene). The CléA certificate should help unemployed individuals who do not have any formal qualification, but who possess relevant workplace skills, to find a job. For employed workers, too, the CléA certificate can enable career progress. Beyond validating basic workplace skills, France has another tool to recognise prior learning (*Validation des Acquis de l'Expérience*, VAE). Participants demonstrate the skills they have acquired through work experience in a jury evaluation, and those who are successful at demonstrating mastery of required skills can obtain a partial or full recognition of a given qualification. Both the CléA and VAE procedures can be supported through the framework of existing training policies, such as the CPF (*Compte Personnel de Formation*). South Africa also has a well-established system for RPL. In place since the start of democracy in 1995, RPL has been important to redress the inequalities created by the apartheid system by enabling validation of skills for those who had been denied access to quality formal education. A new RPL policy for artisans proposes to provide full artisan trade qualifications to non-contracted learners who pass a national trade test—a policy which should help to address shortages in the skilled trades.

Education and training: Policies targeting institutions

To bring about better alignment between the programmes that education institutions offer and the qualifications needed by the labour market, some governments use funding arrangements to steer provision in favour of qualifications or fields of study that are either strategic or in high demand. Some countries set caps on student enrolment by programme, to ensure that supply of graduates does not exceed demand by too much, while other countries use performance-based funding models to link public funding to the employment outcomes of graduates (Box 4.1). Governments can also provide one-off capital funding to higher education institutions to create the necessary conditions for certain skills to be generated. For example, in England, the Higher Education Funding Council of England (HEFCE) distributes public funds to higher education institutions in a way that promotes policy objectives. For example, HEFCE allocated GBP 200 million for the 2015-16 academic year to 73 universities and colleges for development of facilities related to STEM training, as part of the STEM Capital Fund.

Several countries are actively promoting the supply of scarce digital skills by funding education institutions. Digitalisation is changing the types of skills that are in demand in the labour market, and a growing share of jobs is likely to require some level of digital skills. According to the *OECD Skills for Jobs Database*, one of the competencies most in shortage across EU countries is knowledge of computers and electronics. This competency feeds into several shortage occupations, including ICT professionals and ICT technicians. Knowledge of computers and electronics is in particularly high demand in Italy, Spain and France, but also in the United Kingdom. This is consistent with findings from the OECD Survey of Adult Skills showing that about 27% of adults in Italy have poor ICT skills, compared with 23% in Spain, 17% in France, and 10% in England (Figure 4.4). Given these shortages, several countries have introduced initiatives to promote the development of digital skills in schools. For instance, France introduced a digitalisation plan for education, *Plan Numérique pour l'Éducation,* which is to be rolled out over 2015-19 and is built on four pillars: training, resources, equipment and innovation. Teachers receive training on how to use digital tools and how to integrate them into their teaching practices, how to apply digital tools in different disciplines in order to develop new teaching methods, and to understand the current digital culture, including social media. The digitalisation plan also makes digital tools available to schools for use in all fundamental courses. Finally, the plan supports local experimentation on innovative uses of digital tools in teaching. The 2013 Law on Higher Education and Research *(Loi relative à l'Enseignement supérieur et à la Recherche,* Loi ESR*)* also put forward initiatives aimed at more and better use of digital tools in universities. Similarly, Italy introduced a National Plan of EUR 1 billion for the "Digital School" to strengthen the ICT skills of teachers and students and to provide schools with new physical and technological infrastructure and internet connectivity.

Box 4.1. Making higher education provision responsive to labour market demand

Performance-based funding models and performance contracts

From 2017 onwards, **Estonia** will use a new funding model for higher education which will allocate up to 20% of funds based on performance. One of the six indicators used to allocate such funding will be the labour market outcomes of graduates.

In **Denmark** the development contracts signed between the government and institutions include indicators that measure graduate labour market outcomes 4-19 months after graduation. The contracts are not legally binding, but universities must report on their contracts in their annual reports and in the annual audit by the ministry.

Setting caps on higher education

In **Sweden**, higher education institutions use forecasts produced by Statistics Sweden to set caps by programme. While Swedish higher education institutions are generally autonomous in deciding how many students to recruit to their programmes, the Swedish Government sometimes intervenes to make adjustments to these caps based on current and expected skill imbalances (e.g. health and engineering). The Swedish Agency for Higher Vocational Education (*Myndigheten för Yrkeshögskolan*) also determines whether a profession or qualification is in demand by employers and industries, so that VET recruitment remains in line with employer and industry demand.

Finland's National Education Development Plan translates employment forecasts into education needs. These are subsequently used to determine caps on higher education by field of study.

In **Austria**, in order to receive accreditation for new programmes, Austrian legislation requires that Universities of Applied Sciences (*Fachhochschulen*) complete a Demand and Acceptance survey that evaluates the projected demand for each qualification seeking accreditation.

Source: OECD (2016), *Getting Skills Right: Sweden*; OECD (2017), *Financial Incentives for Steering Education and Training*, OECD Publishing, Paris, http://dx.doi.org/10.1787/9789264272415-en.

Figure 4.4. Many adults in Spain, Italy and France have poor ICT skills

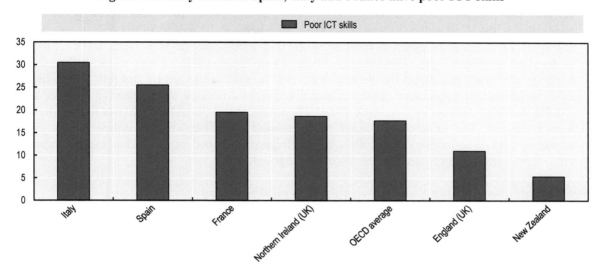

Note: The chart shows the best-performing country (New Zealand), OECD average and reviewed countries included in the survey. The sample includes adults age 25 to 64. Adults are deemed to have poor ICT skills if they report never having used a computer before, or if they were assessed to have insufficient basic computer skills necessary to undertake the computer-based assessment of the survey.

Source: OECD Survey of Adult Skills (PIAAC) 2012.

Policies to activate the unemployed

Policies to activate the unemployed in the labour market are particularly important in countries with high unemployment rates, like South Africa, Spain, Italy and France. Evaluations of training programmes for the unemployed suggest positive employment effects in the medium to long-term, with highest impacts for the long-term unemployed (Card et al., 2015). The type of training that unemployed workers receive also matters. Public employment services can help to ensure that unemployed workers receive training that is relevant to the labour market. Even as decentralisation of active labour market policies (e.g. in Spain and Italy) allows for tailored responses of training programmes to local demand, it can also complicate the co-ordination of public employment services, making it difficult to focus training on skills most in demand nationally. Alternatively, some countries offer employers subsidies to hire and train jobseekers in skills which the employer is having trouble finding in the labour market. Such programmes are shown to be highly successful in activating the unemployed.

Employer subsidies to hire and train low-skilled unemployed generate strong employment outcomes in the United Kingdom and France. In the United Kingdom, the sector-based work academies (SBWA) programme consists of three components: sector-specific pre-employment training of up to 30 hours per week, a work placement and a guaranteed job interview. Employers initiate contact with Jobcentre Plus, the British public employment service, and detail their hiring needs. Jobcentre Plus then provides employers with unemployed candidates and covers the costs of short-term training, which generally lasts three or four weeks. Introduced as a pilot initiative in 2011, the sector-based work academies (SBWA) programme continued following internal evaluations which showed that participation in the programme reduces the time that young jobseekers spend receiving benefits and increases the amount of time they spend in employment (DWP, 2016). Impacts were highest for participants who had been on benefits for 3 months or more prior to the start of the programme. A similar type of programme exists in France, though on an expanded scale. Under the *Préparation Opérationnelle à l'Emploi* (POE), firms receive subsidies for internal or external training when they hire someone who lacks some of the skills required for the job. The subsidy covers a maximum of 400 hours to close the gap between the skills possessed by the new hire and the skills required by the job. While the POE is limited to permanent contracts and fixed-term contracts of at least 12 months, a similar subsidy, *Action de Formation Préalable au Recrutement* (AFPR), exists for shorter-term contracts. The POE can be used by individual firms but also by entire sectors or branches (PO E collective). Over 80% of participants succeed in accessing employment after completing the POE and AFPR training programmes.

Policies to improve matching of skill supply and skill demand

Countries employ a variety of tools to improve the matching of the skills of the unemployed with the needs of the labour market. In Italy, statistical profiling tools were used as part of the Youth Guarantee programme to estimate the risk that young people (age 15-29) might become part of the so-called "NEET" group, i.e. not in employment, education or training. The Italian PES used this information to prioritise services for youth at high-risk of becoming NEET, including providing higher compensation to private employment agencies for matching high-risk youth with jobs, and offering employers larger employment incentives for hiring these young people. Given the success of the use of statistical profiling tools for employing youth, the National Agency for Active Labour Market Policies (*Agenzia nazionale per le politiche attive per il lavoro*, ANPAL) announced its plan to introduce a statistical profiling tool for all PES clients, in order to reduce the burden on PES caseworkers and to respond more quickly and effectively to the needs of jobseekers and employers. Spain also announced its plan to introduce statistical profiling systems in the 2014-2016 Spanish Strategy for Employment Activation (*Estrategica Espanol de Activación para el Empleo*, EEAE). However, while the plan encouraged autonomous communities to introduce statistical profiling systems to better target PES to the specific needs of the unemployed, to date most regions have not done so. France has also taken steps to improve its system for matching the skills of the unemployed with the needs of the labour market. The French PES (*Pôle Emploi*) has been shifting its focus to skills in order to bring about a better alignment between jobseekers and available jobs. Whereas the PES previously matched jobseekers with vacancies based on occupations, a new labour market reference framework helps employers to identify their skill needs and therefore allows the PES to go beyond occupations to match the skill profiles of jobseekers with the skill requirements of vacancies. The labour market reference framework assists employers in identifying their skill requirements for vacancies by suggesting the skills required in similar job postings. This new focus on skills could bring about better matching of jobseekers with jobs.

Box 4.2. Use of statistical profiling tools: Best practice examples

One of the first countries to implement statistical profiling tools for public employment services, **Australia** has been using the *Jobseeker Classification Instrument* (JSCI) since the 1990s. The model predicts the probability of remaining unemployed for longer than 12 months based on the following characteristics: educational attainment, vocational qualifications, English proficiency, age, gender, recent work experience, jobseeker history, country of birth, indigenous status, indigenous location, geographic location, proximity to labour market, access to transport, phone contactibility, disabilities or medical conditions, stability of residence, living circumstances, criminal convictions and other personal factors. Upon client registration, jobseekers complete a questionnaire in order to gather the necessary information to compute their JSCI score. The higher the JSCI score, the higher the risk of long-term unemployment. Jobseekers are classified into one of four streams based on their JSCI score, and this classification determines the amount of funding that case workers may assign to services. Jobseekers in the lowest-risk stream may receive up to AUD 1 232 in services, while those in the highest-risk stream can receive up to AUD 10 000.

In response to a dramatic rise in the unemployment rate and strain on public funds due to rising unemployment income supports, **Ireland** introduced a statistical profiling tool in 2012 to better target public employment services on those with a high risk of entering long-term unemployment. The profiling tool, called PEX (Probability of Exit) and developed in conjunction with the Economic and Social Research Institute (ESRI), predicts the probability that registered jobseekers will exit unemployment within one year based on a model with personal characteristics including: education, basic skills, recent labour market experience, sex, age, number of children, spousal earnings, geographic location, whether living in a rural or urban area, and access to transport. The model is able to predict the correct outcome in 69% of cases. Based on PEX's predictions, jobseekers are segmented into low, medium and high-risk bands, which determine the timing and intensity of intervention:

- Low-risk jobseekers (likely to be unemployed for less than 3 months, approx. 20% of caseload): directed towards self-help tools, and if they remain unemployed for 4 months, they are invited to meet with a caseworker to develop a personalised progression plan.

- Medium-risk jobseekers (likely to be unemployed for 3 to 12 months, approx. 60%): meet with a caseworker within one week of initial engagement session, and subsequently every 3 months to review progress.

- High-risk jobseekers (likely to be unemployed for 12 months or more, approx. 20%): meet with a caseworker within one week of initial engagement session, and subsequently every 2 months to review progress.

Many of the proxies that are currently used to measure skills (e.g. qualifications or occupations) are an imperfect indication of an individual's true skills and competencies. In this context, the **Swedish** PES is working to refine its existing "digital matching tool" to allow both jobseekers and employers to search for each other through a system of skill tags. This focus on skills goes beyond the usual proxies and could enable a better matching of jobseekers to vacancies. Jobseekers can provide information about their qualifications, but also about the specific skills they acquired both formally and informally at work. For example, an IT engineer can advertise skills like C++, Javascript, HTML or PHP. Employers, in turn, can search for specific skills instead of being constrained to search by job title or qualification, which are imperfect proxies for skills. The tool estimates the quality of the match between the jobseeker's attributes and the skills sought by the employer, and generates a ranking of best matches for the employer. Sweden is also developing a system to extract skills tags from the job offers uploaded by employers to the PES system in the form of free text, which is expected to improve the quality of the matching tool.

Source: Statistical Profiling in Practice: International Experiences; European Commission (2016), "Profiling of Jobseekers using Statistical Methods: Ireland"; World Bank Group (2014), "Profiling the Unemployed: A Review of OECD Experiences and Implications for Emerging Economies"; OECD (2016), *Getting Skills Right: Sweden*, OECD Publishing, Paris, http://dx.doi.org/10.1787/9789264265479-en.

Attracting global talent

France and the United Kingdom facilitate entry of high-skilled migrants who have been hired to fill a shortage occupation vacancy. The Global Talent Competitiveness Index (GTCI), produced annually by INSEAD, provides an assessment of how countries compete globally to attract talent. In 2017, the United Kingdom ranked as the third most attractive country in the world in terms of its ability to attract global talent. France came in 24th, followed by Spain and Italy in 35th and 40th places, respectively, and South Africa in 67th place. These rankings largely reflect the ability of educational systems to meet the needs of the economy, and employment policies that favour flexibility, mobility, entrepreneurship and high engagement of stakeholders in business and government. But countries can also influence the supply of skills through migration policy. In the United Kingdom, the Resident Labour Market Test (RLMT) and the Shortage Occupation List (SOL) facilitate entry of skilled migrants. Under the RLMT, employers can bring in immigrant workers to fill a vacancy if they can demonstrate that there is no suitable candidate within the United Kingdom or the European Economic Area to fill the position. High-skilled workers who have a job offer to fill a skill shortage identified by the Shortage Occupation List are exempt from having to pass the RLMT, and their entry is prioritised. The Shortage Occupation List is reviewed periodically by the Migration Advisory Council, which uses a holistic methodology to identify occupations in shortage, relying on both quantitative information (including share of vacancies, changes in wages and changes in employment) and qualitative reports from relevant stakeholders. In France, migration policies also favour entry of migrants with in-demand skills. Employers can bypass the requirement to demonstrate adequate efforts to recruit a suitable candidate on the local labour market for shortage occupations. As in the United Kingdom, this list of occupations in shortage is based on labour market pressure information, and favours inclusion of high-skilled occupations.

South Africa facilitates entry of high-skilled migrants whose qualifications feature on the Critical Skills List, even if they do not yet have a job offer. South Africa recently introduced reforms to attract skilled foreigners. Individuals with skills that feature on the Critical Skills List published by the Department of Home Affairs can apply for a *Critical Skills Visa*. This list is based on a list of occupations in high demand produced by the Department for Higher Education and Training, and it focuses mainly on higher-skilled occupations. The Department of Home Affairs also consults with experts and labour representatives on the occupations that should or should not be on the list. Unlike similar policies in the United Kingdom and France, the Critical Skills Visa in South Africa can be granted to foreign individuals who are qualified to fill a high-demand occupation, even if they do not already have a job offer. In such cases, the initial visa is limited to a 12-month period, during which employment must be secured to obtain renewal. This feature is designed to make South Africa a more competitive destination for skilled foreigners to work.

Policies to boost demand for higher-level skills

Policies that stimulate demand for higher-level qualifications can reduce over-qualification and increase growth and productivity. This policy discussion has focused thus far on examples of policy measures that countries use to bring skill supply into alignment with skill demand. But policy can also influence the demand for skills. Many of the countries reviewed in this note have a large and growing pool of highly-qualified workers. A substantial share, however, is employed in jobs that require a lower level of qualification than the one they have. About 28% of workers in South Africa are over-qualified for their jobs, compared to 21% in Spain and Italy, and 15% in the United Kingdom and France. As a result, many qualifications are not used optimally, reducing the returns on investment in education. Policies stimulating demand for high-qualified workers can address the issue of over-qualification, while at the same time contributing to stronger economic growth and productivity.

For example, technological advancements present an opportunity for economies to engage in higher value-added productive activities and boost demand for higher-level skills and qualifications. Italy, France, Spain and South Africa each have a national plan in place to take advantage of technological change. A key challenge in both Italy and Spain is that small and medium-sized enterprises (SMEs), which comprise the majority of firms in these countries, face constraints in adopting new technologies. For one, it is costly for SMEs to finance adoption of new technology due to lack of economies of scale. Moreover, SMEs may be unaware of the productivity benefits of new technologies. In Italy, *Industria 4.0* is a set of industrial measures with the objective of shifting the Italian productive system towards greater use of new and higher value-added technologies. The measures include: public investment in new technology infrastructure (i.e. Digital Innovation Hubs and Competence Centres); education programmes to boost ICT skills in schools and in the workplace; and provision of better information on the potential of new technologies. The Italian Government designed an awareness campaign to inform employers, especially SMEs, about the potential returns of applying new ICT technologies in manufacturing. The campaign includes training seminars on digital innovation topics, one-on-one consulting services for high-potential SMEs, and a national communication plan supported by newspapers, websites and social media.

Spain's Industria Conectada 4.0 removes barriers to SMEs in adopting new technologies. Similarly, Spain introduced in 2015 an industrial strategy which provides medium-sized manufacturing firms with the information, guidance, and financing they need to harness the benefits of the digital revolution. Called *Industria Conectada 4.0* and managed by the Ministry of Industry, the strategy has three components: an online self-diagnosis tool, a consulting service, and loans. The free self-diagnosis tool allows firms to complete an online questionnaire, and then receive an assessment of their level of digital maturation, which can range from "static" to "leadership." Firms also learn how they compare to similarly-sized firms in the same sector, and the benefits of moving to a higher level of digital maturity in terms of productivity and competitiveness. The consulting service provides more individualised support to firms, and involves preparing a firm-specific action plan. By providing tailored information and support to medium-sized firms, the services remove an important barrier to the adoption of digital technology, which is that SMEs are unaware of the benefits of doing so for productivity and competitiveness.

In France, a new industrial project takes advantage of digitalisation by investing in new technologies and training firms and employees on how to use them. Launched in 2013, the New Industrial France project (*Nouvelle France Industrielle*, NFI) builds on nine industrial solutions: data economy, intelligent objects, digital trust, smart food production, new resources, sustainable cities, ecological mobility, transportation of the future, and medicine of the future. Underpinning the project is the Industry of the Future plan (*Industrie du Futur*), which was launched in 2015 with the objective of modernising the production system in France and supporting industrial employers in dealing with the impact of digitalisation on their business models, their organisation, and their design and marketing practices. A first pillar of the plan is the development of new technologies, and the diffusion of these technologies in French enterprises. Private and public investment in R&D

is at the heart of the development of these new technologies. The second pillar concerns the support for firms to better understand the available technologies, identify obstacles in accessing these innovations, integrate the new concepts and reinvent their economic models. Training of employees constitutes the third pillar, focussing on equipping the next generation of students with the skills needed in new occupations and sectors. The fourth pillar of the plan concerns the visibility and promotion of French technological solutions worldwide.

In South Africa, the New Growth Path framework tries to increase demand for both high and low-level skills. With a target to grow employment by 5 million jobs by 2020, the framework identifies five job drivers: i) direct employment creation through public infrastructure projects, ii) targeting of more labour-absorbing activities across all economic sectors, iii) taking advantage of new opportunities in the knowledge and green economies, iv) leveraging social capital in the social economy and the public services, and v) fostering rural development and regional integration.

Beyond increasing demand for higher-level skills through innovation and job creation policies, countries can also introduce policies to encourage firms to make better use of their employees' existing skills. High-performance working practices (HPWP) characterise work organisation practices (e.g. team work, employee autonomy, task discretion, mentoring, job rotation, and applying new learning) and management practices (e.g. employee participation, incentive pay, training practices and flexibility in working hours) which facilitate greater skill use at work. Only 17% of firms in Italy engage in HPWPs, compared with 20% in France, 25% in Spain and 28% in England (Figure 4.6). In general across OECD countries, policy makers tend to focus on how to boost the supply of skills, and pay relatively less attention to making better use of existing skills in the workplace.

Figure 4.6. High-performance work practices

Share of jobs with high HPWP and mean HPWP score, by country

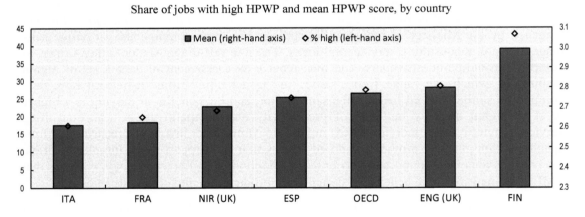

Note: The chart shows the highest performing country, OECD average and reviewed countries included.
Source: OECD Survey of Adult Skills (PIAAC) 2012, 2015.

Box 4.3. Policies to encourage skills utilisation: Examples of good practice

Scottish Funding Council Skills Utilisation Projects

Starting in 2009, Scotland funded twelve projects around skill utilisation, whereby colleges and universities could collaborate with employers to facilitate better usage of skill. Projects were selected by the Scottish Funding Council through a competitive tendering process and included the following:

- The Glasgow School of Art ran a "Creating Cultures of Innovation through Creativity and Design" project that aimed to help business leaders use the skills of their entire workforce to solve business problems by working with a vertical slice of the organisation to help develop a creative thinking process. The method involved holding workshops to brainstorm solutions to a problem facing the firm, with workshop members selected to be broadly representative in terms of their position within the firm, gender, function, age and length of service.

- The Open University in Scotland worked with organisations in the social care sector to make better use of newly-acquired skills of students who had just completed a management level qualification for supervisory staff. Previously, students had complained that when they returned to work after completing this course, their responsibilities did not change, despite their new skills. The Open University helped social care organisations to re-think and broaden the role of students' jobs to more fully use their new skills.

The qualitative evaluation found evidence that universities and colleges can make a positive contribution to skills utilisation, but flagged several issues, including the need to develop expertise in helping organisations to re-think work organisation, job design and their approaches to innovation.

Finnish Workplace Development Programme

A national government programme that ran from 1996 to 2003 (TYKE programme) and continued from 2004 until 2010 with expanded resources (TYKES), the Finnish Workplace Development programme aimed to disseminate good practice and mutual learning around organisational and management practices, models and tools. More than 1,800 development projects were supported in Finnish workplaces between 1996 and 2010, with a focus on innovative solutions to work-related and organisational issues. Qualitative evaluations suggest that the TYKE and TYKES programmes were effective in promoting workplace innovation and productivity.

Source: Keep, E. (2016), "Keep Improving Skills Utilization in the UK: Some reflections on what, who and how"; Oosi, O. et al. (2010), "Ärjen muutoksista työelämän innovaatiotoiminnaksi – Työelämän kehittämisohjelma 2004-10 Arviointiraportti", Tekes Programme Report, No. 5/2010, Helsinki; Arnkil, R. (2003), "The Finnish Workplace Development Programme: A Smalll Giant?", *Concepts and Transformation*, Vol. 9, No. 3, pp. 249-278.

Monitoring and evaluation of policies

Given scarce resources, governments must take into account cost-effectiveness when considering the introduction of a new policy or programme, in addition to its potential to reduce skill imbalances. Robust monitoring and evaluation of policies and programmes can provide policy makers with valuable information about what works, what does not work, for whom, under what conditions and at what cost. Generally, the introduction of new policies or programmes should be preceded by a pilot initiative, whose evaluation can shed light on ways that the implementation of a new policy or programme can be improved and avoid large investment in costly initiatives that do not work. In the countries reviewed, the United Kingdom and France engage regularly in monitoring and evaluation. For example, evaluations were conducted in the United Kingdom for the sector-based work academy programme, Jobseeker's Allowance Skills Conditionality and the employment investment funds; while in France, the *Investissements d'Avenir, Plan 500 000 formations supplémentaires,* and other training programmes for the unemployed (*Aide Individuelle à la Formation, Préparation Opérationnelle à l'Emploi*) were also subject to evaluations. But even in these countries, large-scale policies are not always preceded by a pilot evaluation, e.g. the United Kingdom's new apprenticeship levy. Monitoring and evaluation is less common in Italy, Spain and South Africa.

References

Arnkil, R. (2003), "The Finnish Workplace Development Programme: A Smalll Giant?", *Concepts and Transformation*, Vol. 9, No. 3, pp. 249-278.

Card, D., J. Kluve and A. Weber (2015), "What Works? A Meta Analysis of Recent Active Labor Market Program Evaluations (No. 9236)", Discussion Paper Series", Forschungsinstitut zur Zukunft der Arbeit Institute for the Study of Labor.

DWP – Department for Work and Pensions (2016), "Sector-based Work Academies: A Quantitative Impact Assessment (No. 918)", Research Report, Department for Work and Pensions.

Fernández-Zubieta, A. and T. Zacharewicz (2016), "RIO Country Report 2015: Spain", JRC Science for Policy Report, European Commission.

Keep, E. (2016), "Keep Improving Skills Utilization in the UK: Some reflections on what, who and how".

OECD (2017), *Financial Incentives for Steering Education and Training*, OECD Publishing, Paris, http://dx.doi.org/10.1787/9789264272415-en.

OECD (2016), *Getting Skills Right: Sweden*, OECD Publishing, Paris, http://dx.doi.org/10.1787/9789264265479-en.

OECD (2015), "Non-standard Work, Job Polarisation and Inequality", *In It Together: Why Less Inequality Benefits All*, OECD Publishing, Paris, pp. 135-208, http://dx.doi.org/10.1787/9789264235120-en.

Oosi, O. et al. (2010), "Ärjen muutoksista työelämän innovaatiotoiminnaksi – Työelämän kehittämisohjelma 2004-10 Arviointiraportti", Tekes Programme Report, No. 5/2010, Helsinki.

Statistical Profiling in Practice: International Experiences; European Commission (2016), "Profiling of Jobseekers using Statistical Methods: Ireland".

Stuart, M. et al. (2016), "Evaluation of the Union Learning Fund Rounds 15-16 and Support Role of Unionlearn: Final Report", Centre for Employment Relations Innovation and Change, University of Leeds; Marchmont Observatory, University of Exeter.

World Bank Group (2014), "Profiling the Unemployed: A Review of OECD Experiences and Implications for Emerging Economies".

Chapter 5

Best practices in the design of policies to reduce skill imbalances

Despite the differences between countries in skill-related challenges and policy environments, some consensus has emerged on a set of best practice principles to guide the design of policies to reduce skill imbalances. This chapter presents the most widely-relevant policy recommendations and suggests effective ways to implement them.

Skills have the potential to change lives and drive economies. Highly-skilled adults are more likely than their low-skilled peers to be employed and to hold good-quality and stable jobs. They also tend to earn higher wages and to be more satisfied at work. A high-skilled workforce is also essential for firms to be able to innovate, invest in research development and specialise in high value-added and technologically-advanced industries.

To reap all these potential benefits, it is critical that countries and individuals develop the right skills that respond to labour market needs so that these skills are fully utilised by individuals and employers. Investing in the acquisition of skills during the working life will not achieve the desired effects of promoting innovation and raising productivity and economic growth unless the skills being developed are recognised and used in the labour market. While the decision to acquire certain skills and the choice of field of study do not depend exclusively on the possibility of eventually using them in the labour market, a misalignment between the skills of the workforce and those required by employers will constrain innovation and hamper the adoption of new technologies.

Skill mismatch and shortages entail large costs for individuals, employers and society. Mismatches between the level and field of qualification possessed by workers and those required in their job are pervasive, affecting 34% and 32% of workers in countries included in the *OECD Skills for Jobs Database*, respectively. At the same time, about 40% of employers across 42 countries report facing recruitment problems due to skill shortages, according to the 2016 Manpower Talent Shortage Survey. These types of skill imbalances can result in lower earnings and job satisfaction, higher risk of job loss, loss of competitiveness as well as lower economic growth.

To tackle skill imbalances and minimise the associated costs, it is essential that countries develop effective skills policies based on reliable information on skill needs. Countries need to put in place effective systems for the assessment and anticipation of skill needs and ensure that this information feeds into education, training and labour market policy. Based on the five country-specific policy notes, the previous chapter highlighted examples of good practice in how to tackle skill imbalances. Despite the differences between countries in skills-related challenges and policy environments, some consensus has emerged on a set of best practice principles to guide the design of policies to reduce skill imbalances:

- *Expand opportunities to participate in adult learning.* To adapt to changing skill demand brought about by mega-trends like globalisation, technological change and ageing populations, adults need better opportunities for lifelong learning to upskill and retrain. Rising participation in non-standard working arrangements, like part-time or temporary contracts, creates the need for learning incentives which are not directly tied to one's job. For example, in France, individual training accounts provide rights to training leave which are preserved upon job loss and transferable between employers. In addition to making training incentives portable, training which targets low-skilled workers can help to reduce inherent inequalities in lifelong learning provision, which are apparent across OECD countries. For instance, social partners in the United Kingdom have set up a training fund (*Union Learning Fund)* which actively recruits the participation of low-skilled workers in training activities.

- *Link training for the unemployed to labour market needs.* Training programmes for the unemployed yield the most successful employment outcomes when they are tied closely to the needs of the labour market. One way to ensure that this happens is to focus public spending on training programmes for the unemployed on activities that address identified skill needs, as is done in Finland. Alternatively, governments can also provide subsidies to employers to hire and train the unemployed, which helps to align training for the unemployed with employers' needs. For example, firms in France receive subsidies for internal or external training when they hire a jobseeker who lacks some of the skills required for the job.

- *Recognise informal and non-formal learning.* Validating informal and non-formal learning strengthens individuals' incentives to invest in training, helps to promote job-to-job transitions, and can reduce the incidence of under-qualification. Many underqualified workers have the skills needed to perform their jobs, but may be missing a necessary qualification, perhaps because the educational requirements of their job increased since they were initially hired. Without a qualification certifying their learning, such workers could have difficulty becoming hired by a new employer if they wish to change jobs or if they became unemployed. Recognition of prior learning has been particularly relevant in South Africa, where it has strengthened the signalling power of skills for individuals who had been previously denied access to quality formal education under the apartheid system.

- *Strengthen incentives for employers to invest in training to meet skill needs, but minimise the administrative burden.* Employers have much to gain from investing in the skills of their workforce, including higher productivity and lower turnover. But a number of barriers – information failures, fear of poaching or liquidity constraints – mean actual employer investment in training may be sub-optimal. Government intervention may therefore be warranted, and can include financial incentives to encourage training (e.g. subsidies for work-based learning or to train existing workers), but also tax incentives and training levies. Efforts to encourage employer investment in training need to steer training towards in-demand skills, while avoiding burdensome administrative processes, which can reduce take-up. Small and medium-sized enterprises (SMEs) may be more likely to provide training if they receive assistance in identifying their training needs and developing training plans. For example, in Spain, a pilot initiative provides free technical support to SMEs interested in developing an apprenticeship programme, offering advice on which positions within the company could be filled by an apprentice, and matching available vocational qualifications with the firm's skill needs. Of the 190 firms that were targeted by the consulting programme, 115 planned to offer an apprenticeship the following year.

- *Involve the social partners in vocational education.* Vocational education and work-based learning programmes can deliver skills needed by the labour market, especially where there is strong employer and trade union involvement. Social partner engagement is critical to ensure that the curriculum reflects the needs of the labour market, and that enough work placements are created. For example, in England under the new apprenticeship system, panels of employers (*trailblazers)* will take the lead in setting the curriculum requirements of apprenticeships and establishing their assessment plans.

- *Ensure higher and further education provision is responsive to skill needs in the labour market.* Higher education institutions may be slow to respond to changing skill and qualification demand in the labour market for a number of reasons. Institutions may be reluctant to invest in new teaching and research infrastructure, there may be discrepancies between the courses students want to take and those in demand in the labour market, and the speed of changing skill demand may outpace the development and verification of new qualifications. To reduce the misalignment between skills that are needed by employers and those that individuals acquire, governments can use funding arrangements for education and training institutions to steer the mix of provision in favour of subjects where there is high labour market demand. For instance, the Higher Education Funding Council of England (HEFCE) distributes public funds to higher education institutions in a way that promotes policy objectives, like the development of facilities related to STEM training (STEM Capital Fund).

- *Facilitate labour mobility, particularly the inflow of migrants with skills in high demand.* Enabling labour mobility within a country can reduce skill imbalances by allowing skills and labour to flow to where they are best compensated. Removing barriers to internal labour mobility can therefore help to alleviate shortages and mismatch. For instance, Spain's new nation-wide online job portal, *Empleate*, attempts to remove information barriers to labour mobility by aggregating regional job postings into a single portal. Furthermore, encouraging the entry of foreigners with skills and qualifications which are in high demand can also reduce skill imbalances. For instance, South Africa's *Critical Skills Visa* allows entry of foreigners who are qualified in skills on the country's Critical Skills List, which is based on the list produced by the Department of Higher Education and Training. The Critical Skills Visa can be granted to foreign individuals who are qualified to fill a high-demand occupation, even if they do not yet have a job offer.

- *Stimulate demand for higher-level skills.* Rising educational attainment across OECD countries has not been met, in some cases, with commensurate increases in the demand for higher-level qualifications. As a result, many workers are over-qualified, which represents a pocket of skills that are underutilised and reduces the returns to investment in education. Policies aimed at boosting the demand for higher-level skills can reduce over-qualification, while also contributing to higher productivity, growth, and better job quality and well-being. For example, Italy's *Industria 4.0* proposes to shift the Italian productive system towards greater use of higher value-added technologies, through measures that include: public investment in new technology infrastructure; education programmes to boost ICT skills in schools and in the workplace; and provision of better information on the potential of new technologies.

- *Invest in high-quality skill anticipation and assessment exercises and ensure dissemination and use of information on skill needs in policy making.* Policies to reduce skill imbalances can only be successful if they are underpinned by information about skill needs that is accurate and timely. Most OECD countries engage in some type of skill anticipation and assessment exercise, but there are important differences in the quality of this data and the way it is used. As there are inherent strengths and weaknesses with every type of skill needs data source, drawing from a variety of sources is desirable. For instance, the Migration Advisory Committee in the United Kingdom relies upon both quantitative information (e.g. vacancy, wage and employment data) and qualitative stakeholder reports to assemble its shortage occupation list for migration policy. Skill needs data should also be widely disseminated, both to policy makers and to individuals making human capital investment decisions. For example, the recently-dismantled UK Commission for Employment and Skills previously co-ordinated the production and use of skill needs data in policy making, ensuring that data was made accessible to policy makers. Also, Italy's *Eduscopio* website is a good example of a career guidance website which communicates information about skill needs in the labour market to prospective students in a way that is interactive and easy-to-use.

- *Ensure all relevant stakeholders are involved in the production of information on skill needs.* The involvement of all key stakeholders and the co-ordination of their respective roles are key challenges to overcome to ensure that information on skill needs is used widely and effectively. First, in some countries, key stakeholders (e.g. ministries, public employment services or education providers) are not sufficiently engaged in the collection and use of information on current and future skills needs. In Spain, for instance, limited engagement by senior policy makers has led to scattered policy use mostly at the regional and sectoral levels. In France and South Africa, on the other hand, the central government takes the lead at the cost of more limited use of centrally-collected information at the regional or sectorial level.

- *Strengthen co-ordination mechanisms to ensure that stakeholders work effectively together to assess and use skill needs information.* In some countries these mechanisms are weak or non-existent, leading to limited relevance and use of the information collected. Several examples of good practice are available in this area. Previously, the UK Commission for Employment and Skills played a key co-ordination role in the production of skills intelligence and in fostering responses at the sectoral and regional level through the Sector Skill Councils. Sector Skills Councils also play a key co-ordination role in Canada and the Czech Republic and independent bodies such as national skills advisory groups help improve co-ordination in Denmark, Finland and Germany. A variety of other mechanisms have proven successful in helping to reach consensus, including working groups (e.g. the inter-ministerial skills working groups in United States), or round tables with specific objectives and timelines (e.g. in the Netherlands where they are successfully used to enhance collaboration across regional/sub-regional administrative levels).

- *Engage in regular monitoring and evaluation.* Rigorous evaluation of training programmes helps to improve their design by clarifying what works, what does not work, and under what conditions and for whom. To the extent possible, new policies should be preceded by a pilot initiative, and only expanded if evaluations demonstrate successful outcomes. Building monitoring and evaluation into the design and implementation of training programmes will help to ensure that scarce public resources are used efficiently and effectively.

ORGANISATION FOR ECONOMIC CO-OPERATION AND DEVELOPMENT

The OECD is a unique forum where governments work together to address the economic, social and environmental challenges of globalisation. The OECD is also at the forefront of efforts to understand and to help governments respond to new developments and concerns, such as corporate governance, the information economy and the challenges of an ageing population. The Organisation provides a setting where governments can compare policy experiences, seek answers to common problems, identify good practice and work to co-ordinate domestic and international policies.

The OECD member countries are: Australia, Austria, Belgium, Canada, Chile, the Czech Republic, Denmark, Estonia, Finland, France, Germany, Greece, Hungary, Iceland, Ireland, Israel, Italy, Japan, Korea, Latvia, Luxembourg, Mexico, the Netherlands, New Zealand, Norway, Poland, Portugal, the Slovak Republic, Slovenia, Spain, Sweden, Switzerland, Turkey, the United Kingdom and the United States. The European Union takes part in the work of the OECD.

OECD Publishing disseminates widely the results of the Organisation's statistics gathering and research on economic, social and environmental issues, as well as the conventions, guidelines and standards agreed by its members.

OECD PUBLISHING, 2, rue André-Pascal, 75775 PARIS CEDEX 16
(81 2017 12 1 P) ISBN 978-92-64-27788-5 – 2017